2008   JANUARY   2008

SUN	MON	TUES	WED	THU	FRI	SAT
*	*	1	2	3	4	5
6	7	8	9	10	11	12
13	14	15	16	17	18	19
20	21	22	23	24	25	26
27	28	29	30	31	*	*

CUTTING MA

Danny Calvi
… wears many hats.

What's the best thing that's happened to you this year?
I moved to London.

And the worst?
I moved to London.

What's your guilty pleasure?
Not fit to print.

And what's your New Year's resolution?
Harder, better, faster, stronger.

Laura Clayton
… is learning the ukulele.

What's the best thing that's happened to you this year?
Butlins, Berlin, Brooklyn and back to Butlins.

And the worst?
Roaches.

What's your guilty pleasure?
Vincent Gallo.

And what's your New Year's resolution?
Masterchef—cake division. Grafik waistlines, beware.

Stefan Ketelsen
… is advertising manager at Grafik magazine.

What's the best thing that's happened to you this year?
Finally ditching the car and buying a motorbike instead.

And the worst?
Moving house (again); that's always been my nightmare.

What's your guilty pleasure?
I never really feel guilty about any of my pleasures.

And what's your New Year's resolution?
More pleasure, of course.

Angharad Lewis
… is living in hope of being offered a cuppa.

What's the best thing that's happened to you this year?
July in Ghana.

And the worst?
The rest of the summer in London.

What's your guilty pleasure?
Alice B. Toklas's fudge recipe.

And what's your New Year's resolution?
Empirical research into addiction replacement theory.

Caroline Roberts
… is still in a meeting.

What's the best thing that's happened to you this year?
WSD.

And the worst?
Falling off my WSD.

What's your guilty pleasure?
Corrie—I'm hooked.

And what's your New Year's resolution?
To stop thinking about full suspension.

Grafik would like to thank Arctic Paper, Howard Smith Paper/ Contract Paper and Stones the Printers for sponsoring this issue's Talent section. Special thanks go to John Lee, Roger Warwick and Steve Palmer.

www.arcticpaper.com

www.hspg.com

www.stonestheprinters.co.uk

Grafik Magazine
Third Floor
104 Great Portland Street
London W1W 6PE, UK

+44 (0) 20 7637 5900
hello@grafikmagazine.co.uk

www.grafikmagazine.co.uk

Publisher
Alan Lewis

Editor
Caroline Roberts

Deputy Editor
Angharad Lewis

Staff Writer
Laura Clayton

Sub-Editor
Robert Shore

Designer
Danny Calvi

Advertising Manager
Stefan Ketelsen
+44 (0) 7876 798 762

Distribution
Adam Long
+44 (0) 7961 007 139

Photography
Adam Laycock
+44 (0) 7812 122 949

Fonts
ITC Avant Garde Gothic
Supplied by yellowblack.com

Paper
Arctic Volume by Arctic Paper
Supplied by Howard Smith
Contract Paper

Subscribe to Grafik
0870 428 7957
www.grafikmagazine.co.uk

Grafik is published by Grafik Ltd
Grafik ISSN no. 1479-7534

Speciall thanks to our interns:
Gemma Rhead
Dan Rolfe Johnson

It's just not on that you can't blend pure creative quality, be it branding gurus or artworkers or packaging designers, you-name-it, right down into a smooth liquidy pulp, and then bung them in a tin so you can reach out and get your mitts on them just whenever you fancy. What a shocking disappointing shame.

The nearest thing to it, and it's not far off actually, is the Mustard hotline.

ESSENTIAL THINGS TO SEE AND DO THIS

DECEMBER
JANUARY
ROUGHS

SATURDAY 01
DECEMBER 2007

EASTERN LINE

Elevated to the status of household name thanks to his pared-down Blur portraits, what many people don't know is that there's more to Julian Opie than the two-dimensional. In fact, he's recently turned his hand to the curatorial, and this month sees the unveiling of an exhibition—overseen by Opie—of works by Japanese artist Utagawa Hiroshige. Held at Birmingham's Ikon Gallery, The Moon Reflected is a major retrospective of the nineteenth-century woodblock-printer's work. Featuring several series of vertical prints depicting carefully outlined landscapes and figures, not to mention Hiroshige's sketchbooks, the exhibition reveals a subtle yet beguiling correspondence between both artists' work. See www.ikon-gallery.co.uk for details.

SATURDAY 01
DECEMBER 2007

LEXICAL DEVIANTS

Typophiles ought to head down to East London's Kate MacGarry gallery before 16 December for a group exhibition of five contemporary artists who share a delight in the written word. Signs and Messages from Modern Life features the likes of Stephen Willats, Fiona Banner and Tobias Rehberger and all manner of signage, information theorising, semiotic musings and no doubt provocative language. Visit www.katemacgarry.com for further details.

SATURDAY 01
DECEMBER 2007

GOOD BOOKS

If you're yet to make the trip to the Royal Festival Hall's Poetry Library to see Sam Winston's typographic exhibition, Volume, you've no excuse—not only will you get to marvel at Winston's visual ode to all things linguistic, but it'll cost you nothing for the pleasure. Graphic design, storytelling and illustration intermingle as the complete Oxford English Dictionary (that's a mammoth twenty-one volumes) is folded, page by page, into a serpentine sculpture and Shakespeare's Romeo and Juliet is treated to various aesthetic rearrangements. Head down before 15 January for a visual treat. Go to www.haywardgallery.org.uk for more.

Nirvana
Creative
Production
House

Telephone (T/F)
+44 (0)2078376714
+44 (0)2078378459

Address
14 Rosebery Avenue
London EC1R 4TD
United Kingdom

Online
hello@nirvanacph.com
www.nirvanacph.com

Material Research
Concept Development
Prototyping
Graphic Communication
using bespoke surfaces
Print Production
Luxury Packaging
Outsourcing Solutions
Press Campaign
Retouching
Data Asset Management
3D CAD Drawing
Installations
Brand Experiences
Research & Development

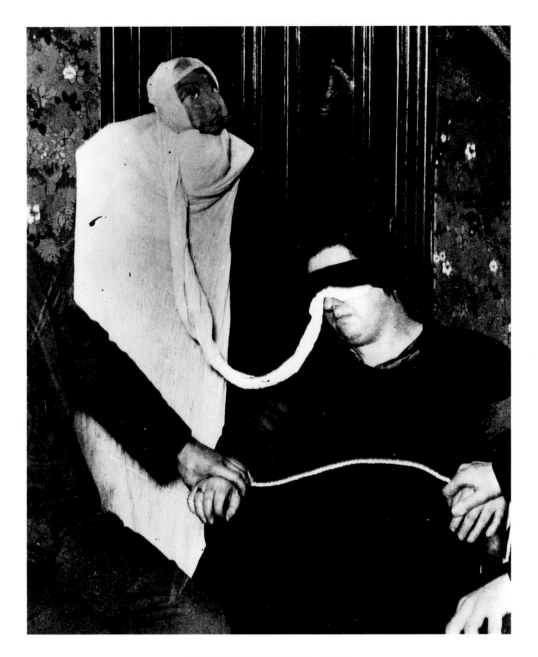

SATURDAY 01
DECEMBER 2007

SMOKE AND MIRRORS

Visitors to the Photographers' Gallery had better keep
their wits about them as curatorial duties have been left
to the otherworldly and unexplained this festive season.
Seeing Is Believing unearths eerie vintage photographs
from the archives of the Harry Price Library of Magical
Literature alongside works by seven artists who harbour
a penchant for the peculiar. Featuring the likes of Fred
Ressler, Susan MacWilliam and Roger Ballen, this
promises to be a show of shivers and surprises. Visit
www.photonet.org.uk to find out more.

FRIDAY 14
DECEMBER 2007

WALL STREET FLASH

Anyone in Amsterdam this month can take a trip to the dark side of 1930s and 40s New York thanks to an exhibition at the city's Foam Fotografiemuseum. Documenting the Big Apple's post-Wall Street Crash deprivation, crime and corruption—through the legendary lens of photojournalist Weegee—the show features over 220 vintage prints. Known to his mother as Arthur Fellig, Weegee was the first photographer to be allowed a police radio in his car, and acquired the title "the famous" thanks to his first-to-the-scene gritty and uncensored high-contrast night shots, developed using a dark room in the boot of his car. More info can be found at www.foam.nl.

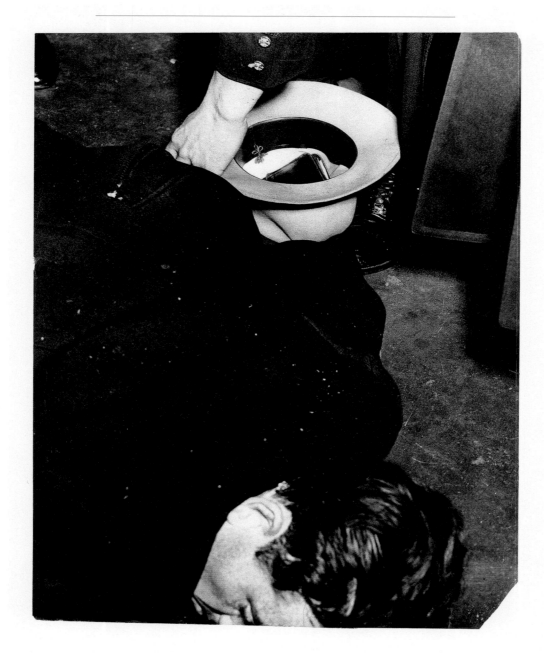

Re-Bag

Limited edition reusable canvas bags

Airside
BB/Saunders
Browns
Design Project
MadeThought
Multistorey
NB: Studio
Non-Format
ODD
Saturday
SEA
Spin
Supermundane
The Designers Republic
Winkreative

Purchase bags at
progresspkg.co.uk/re-bag
or blanka.co.uk

For further information about Progress Packaging
call +44 (0)1484.608.600

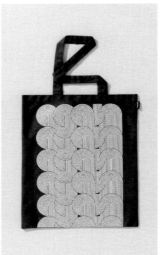

SATURDAY 15
DECEMBER 2007

HACKED OFF

Despite his enviable skills as an artist, musician and DJ, New Yorker Corey Arcangel grants he is first and foremost a computer geek, and a new solo exhibition at Exeter's Spacex gallery has allowed him to indulge in such techie pleasures. The main work, A Couple Thousand Short Films about Glenn Gould, demonstrates Arcangel's 'creative hacking' via a montage of hundreds of YouTube amateur musicians' online performances arranged note by note to a 1741 Bach composition. Grafik suggests any webcam-wielding bedroom guitar strummers make a trip down south to see if they've made an unwitting debut. More information at www.spacex.org.uk.

SATURDAY 15
DECEMBER 2007

FESTIVE FROLICS

If you're dreading the thought of playing Santa for those hard-to-please designer pals, fret not, help is at hand in the shape of Somerset House's Design Grotto. For two days only, the design community's great and good will set up shop providing workshops, affordable Xmas treats and all manner of creative tomfoolery. Visitors can add their Christmas list to the mammoth paper chain installation, get stuck into badge-making or indulge in a little chocolate typography, and what's more it's all in the name of charity. Head down on 15 (6pm—11.30) and 16 December (11am-6pm) and don't forget to stop by Grafik's stall for a mince pie. See www.thedesigngrotto.com for more info.

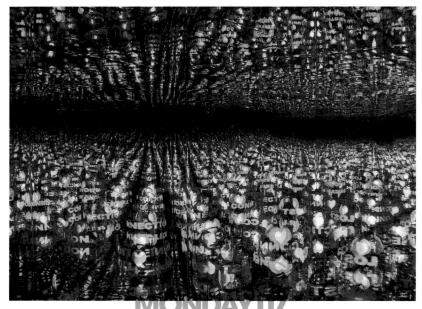

MONDAY 07
JANUARY 2008

GLASS DANCE

Contrary to popular assumptions that he's "a Russian from the moon", artist Andrey Bartenev claims to hail from Venus, and—what's more—if he wasn't causing a global stir in the art world, he'd rather like to be a dancing pianist. Lucky, then, that his latest work, on show at London's Riflemaker gallery, is more than a little bit disco-infused. Featuring a dancefloor of revolving, mirrored light spheres, endlessly relaying the words "disco" and "nexion", the work aims to evoke personal strife in a world of endless communication. See for yourself from 7 January.
Go to www.riflemaker.org for more.

FRIDAY 18
JANUARY 2008

COLOUR THERAPY

If the post-holiday blues have set in come New Year, Grafik recommends a sojourn to Amsterdam's Stedelijk Museum. Thanks to German artist Ulla von Brandenburg, a healthy injection of colour has swept into the gallery's Docking Station space in the form of a labyrinthine installation. With a 16mm film at its core—taking viewers into the equally warren-like confines of a baroque castle—the maze of fabric-clad panels is inspired by the colour schemes of the Bauhaus and the Lüscher Colour Test. Head down to get a little lost before 24 February.
See www.stedelijk.nl for more.

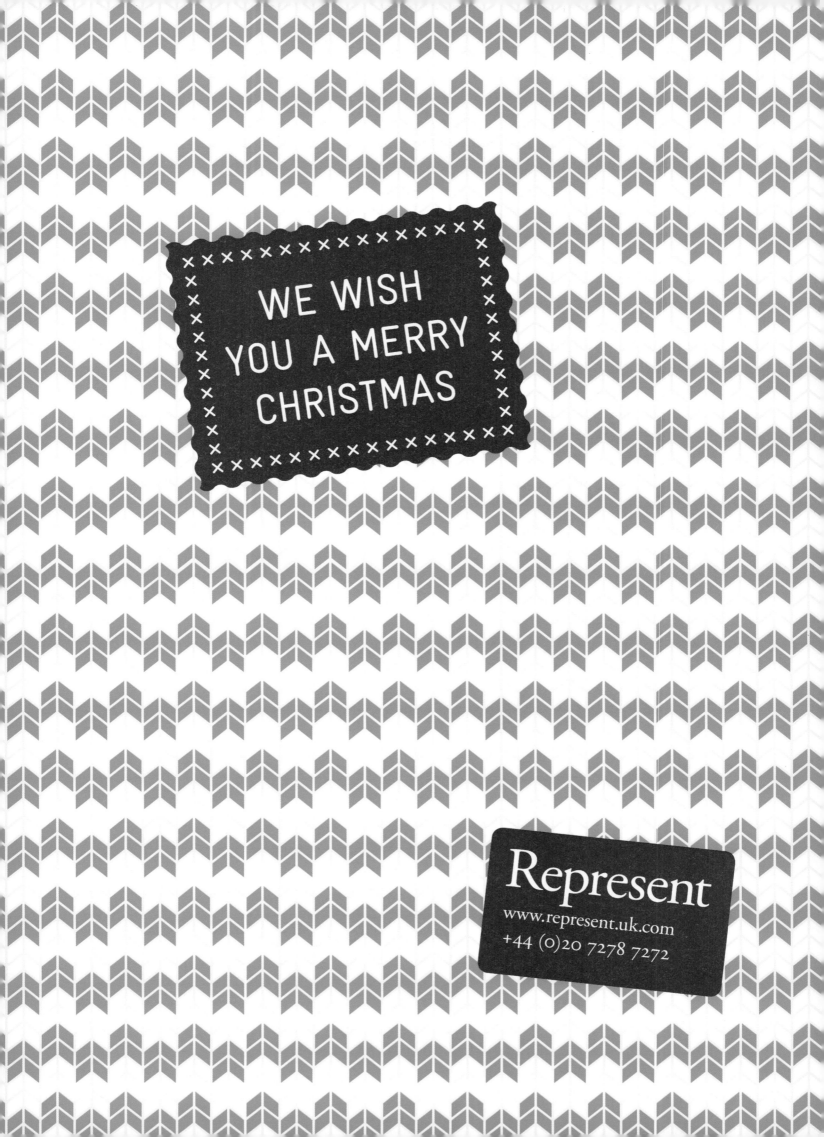

2007

MADE BY YOU

6

TI

i6

Welcome to Grafik's annual celebration of the greatest graphic design work of the last twelve months. The public spotlight has fallen briefly but brightly on graphic design twice in 2007: Helvetica hit the big time to rave reviews in the national press, and logo design made it onto breakfast TV, thanks to the 2012 debacle.

Meanwhile all you hard-working designers have been getting on with creating some truly inspiring and innovative graphics. On the following pages we celebrate your endeavours. First up is Grafik's Top Twenty, where we salute the projects that have surprised and delighted us most this year.

Then turn to pages 38 to 81, to find out what's been making Grafik's friends and contributors green with envy and pink with admiration during 2007. Here's to a year of magnificent work. We hereby lay down the gauntlet for more in 2008…

ADAM LAYCOCK
PHOTOGRAPHY

DANNY CALVI
ART DIRECTION

Mapac

www.mapac.com

CLASS OF 2007– GRAFIK CHOOSES THE DEFINITIVE WORK FROM THE PAST YEAR

BIBLIODYSSEY
BY FUEL

Did you know that the word 'silhouette' is taken from the name of Etienne de Silhouette, a miserly French finance minister whom people mocked in the 1760s for wearing black in the street? Neither did we—until we picked up a copy of Bibliodyssey, one of the most riveting books of 2007. Designed and published by Fuel, this is a cornucopia of the strange and bizarre; a compendium of the online work of the enigmatic 'PK', who has spent years exploring obscure corners of the internet, harvesting images of book illustrations from online archives. The resulting collection—what he dubs "materia obscura"—is a toothsome visual feast, sometimes beautiful, often sinister, that shines a light into the dustiest corners of human history. We've also been addicted to the regularly updated online version at:

bibliodyssey.blogspot.com

WIELS
BY SARA DE BONDT

We profiled Sara De Bondt in issue 157 this year and it was very satisfying to have a lady on the cover of Grafik for a change. Sara's had quite a year and has established herself as a shining beacon on the independent graphics scene. One of the highlights of 2007 for us has been the unfolding story of her work for Wiels contemporary art centre in Brussels, which she described in detail in our Case Study in July. She has been responsible for the development and implementation of the entire Wiels identity—no mean feat and one that will keep evolving into 2008. Look out for more exciting work from Sara's studio in the new year, including, hopefully, some exhibition curatorship from the lady herself.

www.saradebondt.com

FONT CLOCK
BY SEBASTIAN WRONG

How can something so Wrong be so right? One of the first and most important rules that's drummed into wet-behind-the-ears graphic design students is that they should never use more than two typefaces at a time. However, rules are there to be broken, especially when such wilful typographic abuse results in an object as drop-dead gorgeous as Sebastian Wrong's Font Clock. Manufactured by Established and Sons, this instant design classic features no fewer than twelve different typefaces, all of which appear in sequence in this witty but oh-so-stylish take on the twenty-four-hour clock. If you're listening, Santa, we've been very, very good girls at Grafik this year (honest)...
www.establishedandsons.com

OVERLY CHLOË
BY SELF SERVICE

If there's one lady we don't mind having emblazoned lifesize on the walls of Grafik Mansions, it's Chloë Sevigny. Of course, the fact that she's also typographically adorned, thanks to Work in Progress and its Overly Chloë spring/summer issue of Self Service magazine, scores her further points in the design credibility stakes. Thanks to her faultless cool, enviable wardrobe and excellent career choices, Miss Sevigny earned herself an entire issue of the biannual fashion bible, and an embossed and hard-backed one at that. Produced alongside a poster series of gigantic Chloë images, each with its own custom typographic ode, this is one mag that certainly won't be leaving Grafik's coffee table.
www.workinprogress.com

White and blue chiffon shirt, Roberto Cavalli denim top left.

I'VE BEEN A
DDICTED TO
GRAY CARDIG
ANS SINCE H
IGH SCHOOL

PHOTOGRAPHY BY TERRY RICHARDSON STYLING BY CAMILLE BIDAULT-WADDINGTON
*QUOTE FROM HOUSE & GARDEN, JANUARY 2007

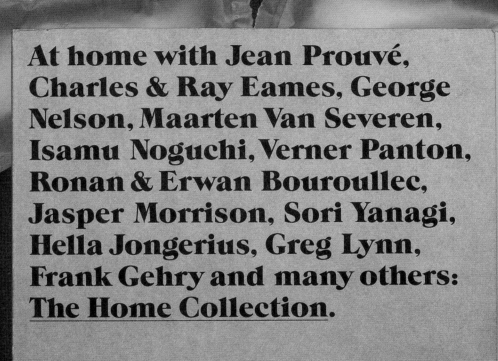

**At home with Jean Prouvé,
Charles & Ray Eames, George
Nelson, Maarten Van Severen,
Isamu Noguchi, Verner Panton,
Ronan & Erwan Bouroullec,
Jasper Morrison, Sori Yanagi,
Hella Jongerius, Greg Lynn,
Frank Gehry and many others:
The Home Collection.**

vitra.

VITRA HOME COLLECTION
BY CORNEL WINDLIN

Furniture catalogues don't generally get the Grafik pulse racing, but when it's from Vitra and it's designed by Cornel Windlin, it's a completely different matter. This year's Home Collection catalogue doesn't disappoint— it features the usual mix of casually styled aspirational interior (and exterior) shots, interspersed with factory shots, and is printed on various different stocks using both four-colour and black and white. Windlin roped in a selection of artists to create an off-the-wall scrapbook based on archive images, there's a tongue-in-cheek puzzle section, as well as a poster featuring a decidedly scary furniture monster—furniture-based fun for all ages. Look out for Windlin's excellent new book Project Vitra, published by Birkhauser, out now.
www.lineto.com

DAVID THORPE
BY JOHN AND ORNA DESIGNS

In artist David Thorpe's work, past and future fuse into a world hovering between reality and fantasy. We were totally seduced by this catalogue of Thorpe's latest exhibition—The Defeated Life Restored—by John and Orna Designs, because it does precisely the same thing. If it weren't for its pristine condition, you might expect to discover it, with its cloth-bound cover, silver-embossed type, thick creamy paper stock and tipped-in plates (of his fictitious botanical studies), on a creaking antique bookstore shelf somewhere. The meticulously constructed architectural installation of carved wood and glass at the core of Thorpe's exhibition is recreated sculpturally in the book with die-cut, gate-folded endpapers and the book's type is a recreation of the archaic hand-painted lettering in Thorpe's works. This is time-travel in book form and earns a dust-gathering place of honour on the Grafik shelves.
www.johnandornadesigns.co.uk

ANCIENT AND MODERN
BY APFEL

Just a small London gallery and only a year old, Ancient and Modern has nonetheless been the venue for some of the city's most captivating shows in 2008. Only fitting, then, that these exhibitions should be accompanied by some of the best art-related graphic ephemera to flit through the Grafik letterbox in 2007. The attention to detail, diminutive stature and beautiful materials that APFEL have apportioned to the flyers, invites and leaflets for each show make them feel like missives to treasure and keep and we paid fitting homage to them in issue 148's Art Special Report. There's a taste of the past in the papers, fonts and processes, which perfectly echoes the gallery's location in one of the most richly historical parts of town. Well worth visiting (and, of course, signing up to the mailing list).

www.apracticeforeverydaylife.com, www.ancientandmodern.org

OFOFFJOFF
BY JULIA BORN

When is a look-book not a look-book? When it's also a series of lifesize posters and a piece of performance in graphic disguise. Julia Born and regular collaborator JOFF executed our favourite fashion/graphics double entendre this year with OFOFFJOFF: ONE TO ONE, featured as a Case Study in issue 150. Fashion designer JOFF's collection was a solipsistic endeavour, with each one-off garment conceived in his image, produced in his size and sold only to friends and fans directly after his 'performance' of them. The book, then, is fittingly JOFF-centric and as close to a paper embodiment of a person as you can get—ten lifesize portraits (by Anuschka Blommers and Niels Schumm), chopped up, piled up and bound in a fabulous typograpic cover. A fashion oroboros moment we couldn't help but admire...

www.joff.nl

BE LONG A PART
BY HELGA STEPPAN AT MAN&EVE GALLERY

The simple genius of Helga Steppen's exhibition at Man&Eve gallery this year was a eureka moment. The photographer's colour series—her possessions arranged by hue—gave us a whole new perspective on tidying-up, not to mention being an artful and rather beautiful exploration of ideas about collectorship and the beauty of ordinariness. Also on show was an installation made entirely of transparent objects—all possessions lent by Helga's friends and acquaintances. Here they became anonymous elements of a united whole but also emblems of individual, untold stories about a network of relationships. We also tip our hats to Matilda Saxow, responsible for Man & Eve's excellent identity and ephemera this year. For Helga's exhibition it's next stop New York and Matilda is sallying forth as an independent London designer. Bonne chance, ladies.

www.manandeve.co.uk

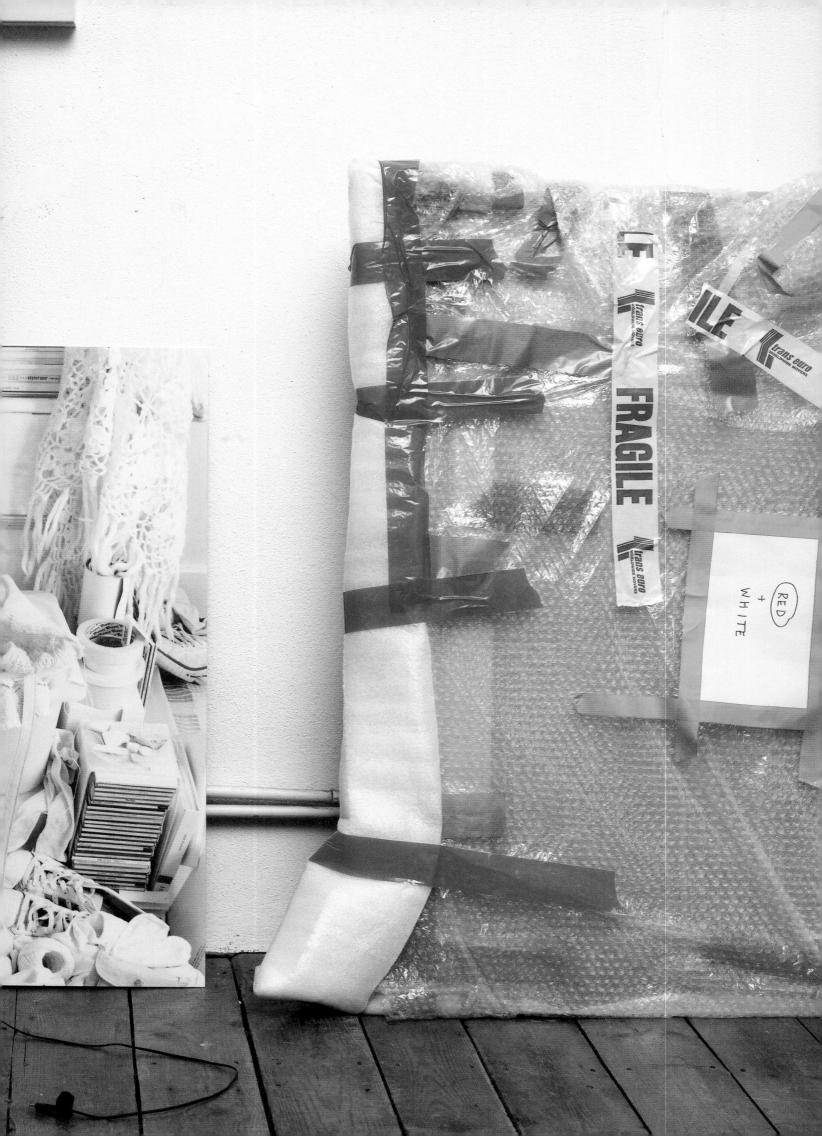

ACNE PAPER, SPRING/SUMMER 07
BY ACNE

A bit like Diesel but about a zillion times cooler, Acne is much more than just a purveyor of fine jeans to the fashion cognoscenti. To service all its creative endeavours there's Acne Digital, Acne Films and Acne Creative, and this handsome oversized biannual magazine is the result of a collaboration between all three. To call it a promotional magazine would be underselling it—as well as a visual treat, it's a quality read with some fine contributors from the worlds of art, fashion and design. The fourth issue took playfulness as its theme and featured contributions from, among others, Grafik favourite Rachel Thomas. With longtime cohort photographer Dan Tobin Smith, Thomas created a series of intriguing three-dimensional typographic vignettes paying (playful) homage to some of her favourite artists. Picasso would definitely have been impressed.

www.acnepaper.com

TYPEWRITTEN PORTRAITS
BY NADINE FAYE JAMES

A little bit of hand-craftery amidst the ether of digital-fuelled design never fails to raise a few 'oohs' and 'aahs' in the Grafik office. However, this year's analogue award by far and away goes to Nadine Faye James. Blessed with an unfathomable knack for drawing five-minute punctuation-mark portraits using a hefty Alder typewriter, James has proven a sensation at weddings, bar mitzvahs and design events this year. Typing straight onto till roll, she produces two copies—one for the sitter and another to collate, duplicate and bind into charming runs of little books. And if that's not enough, she also responds to emails via handwritten letter. Swoon.

www.nadinefayejames.co.uk

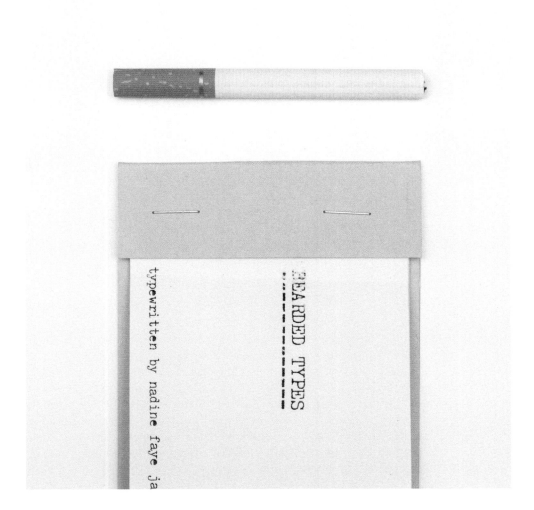

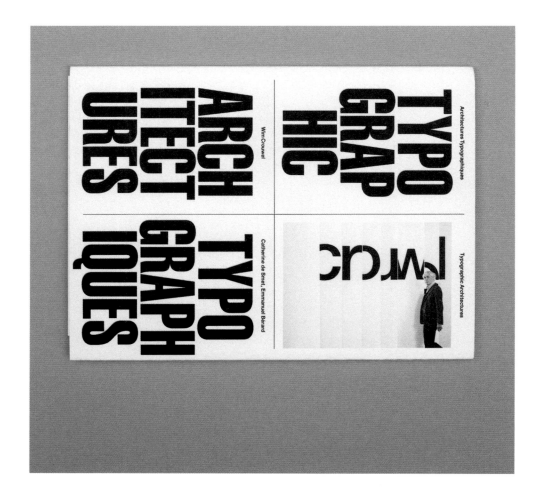

ARCHITECTURES TYPOGRAPHIQUES
BY EXPERIMENTAL JETSET

While the design hordes flocked to Wim Crouwel's D&AD lecture in London this summer, the really hot ticket was for the opening of his exhibition Architectures Typographiques (1956–76) at Galerie Anatome in Paris. The exhibition brought together some of Grafik's favourite Amsterdammers, as Experimental Jetset were asked to create the catalogue and all the supporting promotional material. Jetset's succinct yet striking typographic solution (inspired by the title of the show) managed to avoid any Crouwel-esque pastiches, and the beautifully crafted accompanying catalogue was equally restrained, letting the work (and the great man) speak for itself. You can help Mr Crouwel celebrate a very significant birthday next year by visiting 80I80, an exhibition to be staged in London next autumn.

www.experimentaljetset.nl

FORMS OF INQUIRY
BY ZAK KYES

In London's best graphic design show of the year by a long chalk, super-talented Zak Kyes brought together nineteen of the most exciting graphic designers from around the world under the roof of the Architectural Association. This was a chance to see how the likes of Julia Born, Mevis and van Deursen, James Goggin and Will Holder went about researching and responding to architecture through graphic design. We'd expect nothing less than such a coup from Zak: as well as his own studio, he also runs the AA print department, spiriting up with seeming effortlessness—and startling frequency— an endless round of typographically inspiring and graphically innovative ephemera for the AA. If you didn't make it to the show (shame on you), then the excellent catalogue is the next best thing. Also revisit Grafik's review of the exhibition in issue 157. We look forward to more from Zak Group in 2008…

www.zak.to

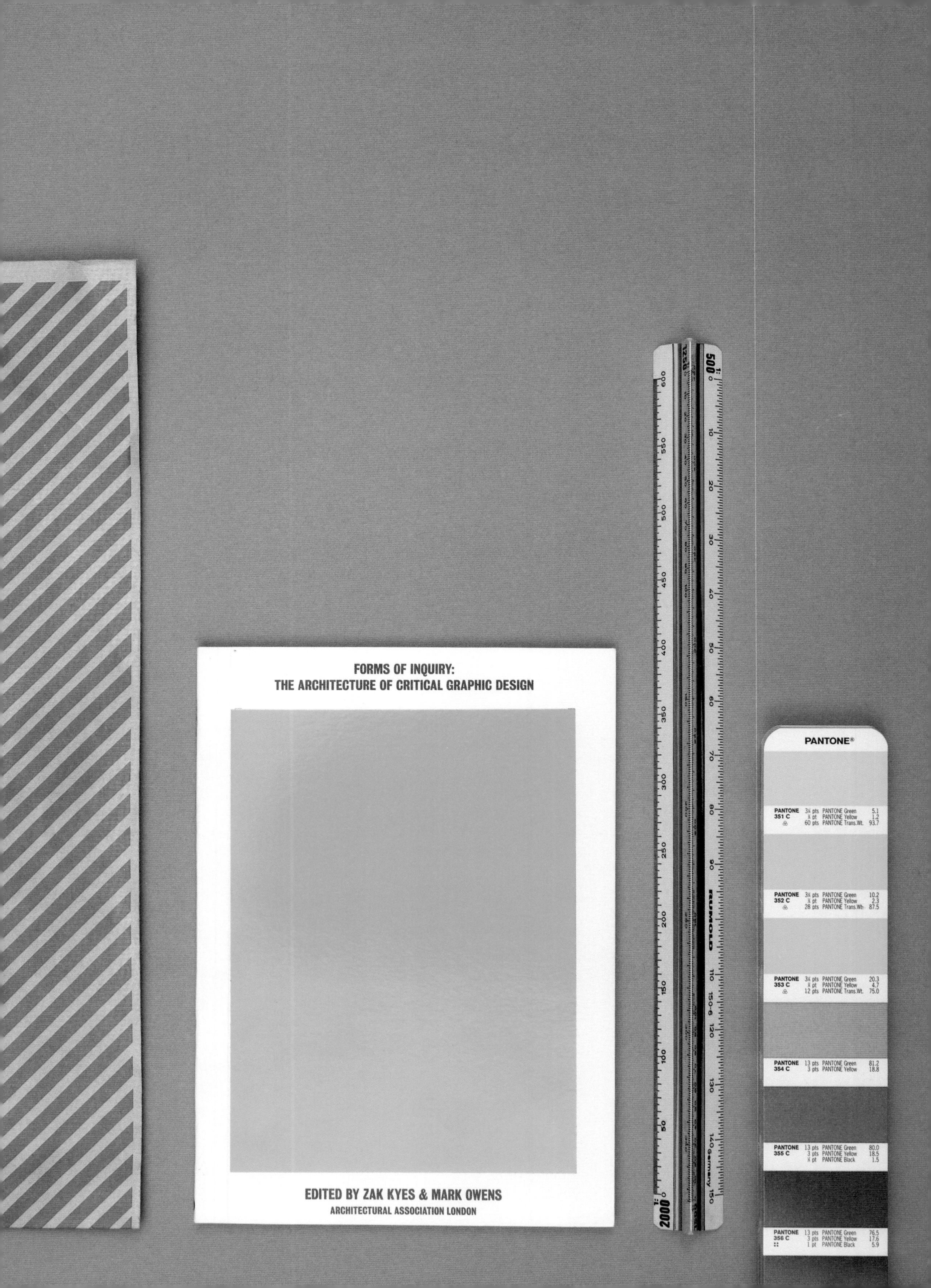

FORMS OF INQUIRY:
THE ARCHITECTURE OF CRITICAL GRAPHIC DESIGN
EDITED BY ZAK KYES & MARK OWENS
ARCHITECTURAL ASSOCIATION LONDON
RUMOLD
PANTONE®
PANTONE 351 C
PANTONE 352 C
PANTONE 353 C
PANTONE 354 C
PANTONE 355 C
PANTONE 356 C

N-D-S-M
MAGAZINE
NON-PROFIT
ISSUE #1.4

A NON-PROFIT ORGANIZATION
IS AN ORGANIZATION WHOSE
PRIMARY OBJECTIVE IS TO SUPPORT
SOME ISSUE OR MATTER OF PRIVATE
INTEREST OR PUBLIC CONCERN
FOR NON-COMMERCIAL
PURPOSES.

NON-PROFIT   ISSUE #1.4

NDSM

Issue #1.1 Modula

N-D-S-M MAG
BY JENS SCHILDT AND MATTHIAS-JENS KREUTZER

A hearty slap on the back is in order for Rietveld alumni Jens Schildt and Matthias-Jens Kreutzer for producing one of the best graduate projects Grafik has seen this year. N-D-S-M magazine takes a four-issue look at the communities living in Amsterdam's NDSM Wharf. Accommodating over two hundred studios, events venues and even a skate park, NDSM produces a huge output of posters and flyers which Schildt and Kreutzer aimed to unite. The resulting magazines address the theme Non-Profit via three different aspects: space, people and ideals, with the fourth and final larger publication reviewing its preceding numbers. With each taking a different format and aesthetic approach, be it typographic, photographic or material-led, the complete set spells a dedicated and striking solution. Keep up the good work, boys.

schilla77@hotmail.com

HARD SCHOOL BOOKS
BY THE RIETVELD ACADEMIE

If they're not already sitting proudly on your bookshelf, we suggest that Rietveld Academie and Veenman Publisher's Hard School Books feature high up on your Christmas list this year. Comprising six natty volumes to answer pretty much everything you've ever wanted to know about being a designer but were afraid to ask, Hard School Books tell it like it is, from plagiarism to email etiquette to the pay roll. Each sporting a different typographic style (Talks about Money is set out entirely in speech bubbles, while I Heard They Ripped It Off is scrawled by hand), once laid side-by-side in the correct order they come together thanks to a defiant spray-painted black line spanning all six covers. Top marks again to Rietveld for these self-schooling gems.

www.gerritrietveldacademie.nl, www.veenmanpublishers.com

PROJECTION FOR TODAY'S ART FESTIVAL
BY MAXALOT

We're not quite sure how they manage it, but we're very jealous of Maxalot. As well as running a graphic design gallery in Barcelona and producing a collection of designer wallpapers and prints, founders Max and Lotje seem to spend most of the year gadding around the world mounting a series of supercool exhibitions. 2007 was no exception, Grafik's favourite being a stunning projection based show that formed part of the fourth Today's Art expo in The Hague. The City Hall building became a massive blank canvas, with twenty-four artists (including usual suspects Build, Eboy and Universal Everything) seeing their work light up the night sky, with the added excitement of live drawing. Look out for Maxalot's second gallery, due to open in an "unexpected spot" in Amsterdam next year.
www.maxalot.com

TYPOGRAPHIC MASONRY INSTALLATION
BY RICHARD NIESSEN

All hail Dutchman Richard Niessen for one of this year's most creative approaches to type. Renouncing the minutiae more often associated with the typographer's toil, Niessen thinks big, so much so that his long-term project Typographic Masonry has spawned an entire city. Showcased at Chaumont's Chapelle des Jésuits last June, and exhibited at the Stedelijk museum in the Autumn, TM-City is a techi-colour metropolis of Niessen's graphic output, featuring stacked flyer skyscrapers, poster parks and streets named after design heroes. "My goal is to tell a more abstract, non-referring story than is usual in today's 'Dutch Design,'" he explains. And succeed he does.
www.tm-online.nl

SANG BLEU

sang bleu tattoo journal
issue zero

K2 IDENTITY
BY SEA

Most jobs include a degree of client arm-twisting as far as special materials, prints and processes go—budgets exist for the sole purpose of being squeezed, don't they? One job that didn't present such a problem was SEA's vibrant and tactile identity for longtime collaborators K2, the only sensible option for self-respecting designers in need of a bit of top-quality screenprinting. Of course, the real skill in a job like this is knowing when to stop, and SEA's fluid designs, applied across the whole range of K2's collateral, strike the perfect balance between excitement and excess. K2 repaid the favour later in the year when they (perhaps foolishly) agreed to print (by hand) the entire print run of Grafik's 150th issue, creating over 12,000 individual works of cover art.
www.seadesign.co.uk, www.k2screen.co.uk

SANG BLEU
BY MAXIME BUECHI

2007 saw team Grafik come very close to making some permanent aesthetic changes, and we're not talking mag design. When Maxime Buechi's very coffee table-friendly ode to tattoo artistry, Sang Bleu magazine, arrived on our doormat, some serious inking envy came into play. Celebrating not just handsome tattoo designs, but the individuals who brandish them, Sang Bleu is as much a photography portfolio and typographic showcase as a source of indulgence for tattoo fanatics. Destined to become a classic, we strongly suggest you track one down, perhaps however at the peril of any unblemished skin.
www.sang-bleu.com

THOUSAND
BY PHILIP-LORCA DICORCIA

Less a book, more a page-turning adventure through a paper mountain range, Philip-Lorca diCorcia's Thousand is our book of the year in terms of visual escapism. Published by the unstoppable Steidl (purveyors of some of the finest books we see year-on-year), Thousand tells a photographic story that feels deeply cinematic. DiCorcia's photographs have a vernacular or documentary feel and look like they're moments caught by chance—in fact, they are all carefully composed and lit tableaux. Far from a simple coffee-table monograph, this is a project where the book format is used as a narrative device, whose physical properties—soft cover and wide spine that allow the book to open flat, pages of lightweight uncoated stock—create a metronomic, temporal looking experience: you flip pages like seconds ticking on a clock or frames flickering in a film.
www.steidlville.com

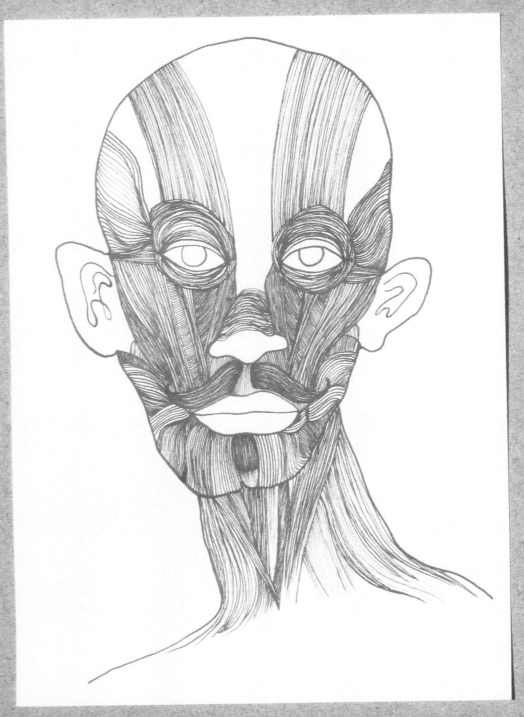

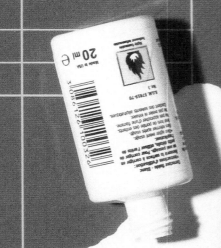

2007
WHAT MADE IT FOR US

GRAFIK'S FRIENDS AND CONTRIBUTORS REVEAL THE GRAPHIC-RELATED PEOPLE, PROJECTS AND EXPERIENCES THAT HAVE IMPRESSED THEM MOST THIS YEAR.

JOP VAN BENNEKOM
FANTASTIC MAN

SARA DE BONDT

JOE BURRIN
THIRD EYE DESIGN

KJELL EKHORN
NON-FORMAT

EXPERIMENTAL JETSET

JON FORSS
NON-FORMAT

MARTIN FROSTNER

WILLIAM HALL

RICHARD HOGG

COREY HOLMS

HUDSON POWELL

BEN PARKER
MADETHOUGHT

TOM PHILLIPS
EXPOSURE

DAVID QUAY
DAVID QUAY DESIGN

DANNY SANGRA

JENS SCHILDT

BECKY SMITH
LULA MAGAZINE

FRAUKE STEGMANN

STUDIOTHOMSON

CHARLIE THOMAS

RACHEL THOMAS

ERIK TORSTENSSEN
SATURDAY

ROBERT URQUHART
DESIGNERS ARE WANKERS

MATT WILLEY
STUDIO8

YES STUDIO

Spread from LeGun 3 by
Bill Bragg

'News' by Bill Bragg

Faithful by Mario Hugo

ILLUSTRATION

BENOIT PLATÉUS

He's not really an illustrator, more an artist, but he makes a really brilliant series of self-published, xeroxed zines, called One Inch Off. I'm working on a book of his drawings at the moment, and am a big fan of his obsessive doodling.
(Sara De Bondt)
www.baronianfrancey.com

HELLOVON

Good old traditional craftsmanship developed and transformed into surprising, cool and contemporary compositions. (Kjell Ekhorn)
www.hellovon.com

GEOFF MCFETRIDGE

A while ago we visited Bend the Void, an exhibition by Geoff McFetridge that took place in art space Mu (Eindhoven), and we were very impressed by it. It was such a good installation, featuring hidden rooms, hypnotic animations and amazing
sculptures; it really was an overwhelming experience. The real stars of the show were Geoff McFetridge's drawings: abstract landscapes, surreal characters, poetic posters.
McFetridge's art seems to refer to the 'soft modernism' of 60s and 70s 'self-help' book covers, and the eerie psychedelic realms of Eastern European animation movies. But somehow he manages to take these references and turn them into a completely new language.
(Experimental Jetset)
www.championdontstop.com
www.mu.nl

MARIO HUGO
TOMOKAZU MATSUYAMA
SAEKO TAKAGI

Mario Hugo (aka Loveworn) for great draughtsmanship, experimentation and seemingly infinite patience—have you seen his embroidered type?
I'm also very keen on the work of Tomokazu Matsuyama and also Saeko Takagi, both of whom make me want to be far more daring with colour, but strictly speaking they're both fine artists.
(Jon Forss)
www.loveworn.com
www.saekotakagi.com

HIROSHI KARIYA

Hiroshi Kariya is making nice, surreal, sensitive drawings and arranging clubnights with funny names. (Martin Frostner)
www.hiroshikariya.co.uk

MARCH CASTLE

(Richard Hogg)
www.needleandlead.co.uk/

MARIO HUGO

Mario Hugo's illustrations are amazing to begin with, but he then works in multiple media, from traditional pencil and ink to embroidery. He works for larger corporate clients, but still manages to retain his own voice. (Corey Holms)
www.loveworn.com

NICOLA PECORARO

Nicola is a friend of ours who is producing skilled and thoughtful work. Always grounded in an amazing ability to draw but never relying on this as a sole means to communicate. Beautiful stuff...
(Hudson Powell)
www.hopaura.org

GRRR

(Ben Parker)
www.grrrr.net

SEBASTIEN AGNEESSENS

He isn't an illustrator but I am interested in the approach of curator Sebastien Agneessens. Sebastien is a new breed of curator whose mission is to sabotage the boundaries between brands and art. Like all good revolutionaries he was trained by both sides in his ascendancy, working at Chanel and Armani before opening his own gallery in downtown New York. His recent work for Diesel, Starbucks and Lexus is very rad. (Tom Phillips)
www.formavision.info

KOEWEIDEN POSTMA

I'm not a user of illustration. I really do not know what's going on, but I do like the illustrations from Koeweiden Postma inviting you to eat with a Muslim family during the month of Ramadan.
(David Quay)
www.koeweidenpostma.com

ROB MCNALLY

Artist, illustrator—whatever he is Rob McNally is the best of 2007 and will probably be the best of 2008 too. (Danny Sangra)
www.myspace.com/robertmcnally

KALLE MATTSSON

(Jens Schildt)
www.hijackyourlife.com

KLAUS HAAPANIEMI

The Taika line of ceramics launched this year for littala are the tip of the iceberg of his burgeoning oeuvre. One to watch. (Charlie Thomas)
www.klaush.com
www.iittala.com

TASHA AMINI

I am a fan of Tasha Amini's work. She seems to have a thing about bows, which she also made in clay and hung in the space at East, so it became part of the detail of the room, like a bit of ornamentation. There is a decorative element that crops up a lot in her work but it's always mediated by humour or melancholy or something else, something that stops it being just that. Here it's the play between the pretty decorative feel of the bow and the strict monochrome, almost Op Art-like lines that feels like a weird but oddly attractive collision of styles and ideas. (Rachel Thomas)
www.katemacgarry.com/tashaamini

JESPER WALDERSTEN

Chic grown-up simplicity with humour.
(Erik Torstensson)
www.jesperwaldersten.com

SARA CULLEN

A recent graduate from Manchester, sensitive, sinister deco, on the way somewhere.
(Robert Urquhart)
web.mac.com/catandfoxadventures

BILL BRAGG

Wonderful, wonderful stuff. Intriguing, surprising and beautiful. Engaging in the way that great illustration ought to be. He's completely unaffected by commercial whims and he has a fantastic sense of humour. For me he's as good as it gets. He's also a brilliant bloke. (Matt Willey)
www.legun.co.uk

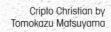

Cripto Christian by
Tomokazu Matsuyama

Bacteria by March Castle

Cranes by
Klaus Haapenemi

Quote for Channel 4's
35th anniversary book by
Mario Hugo

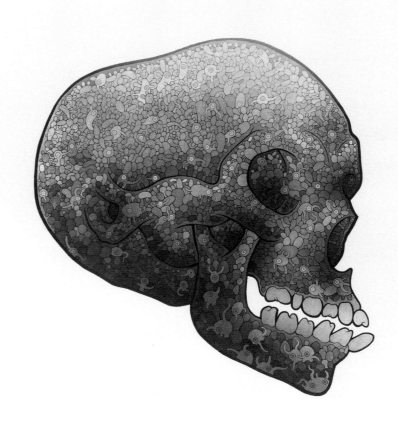

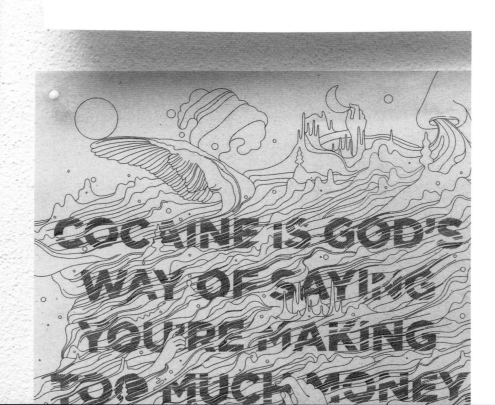

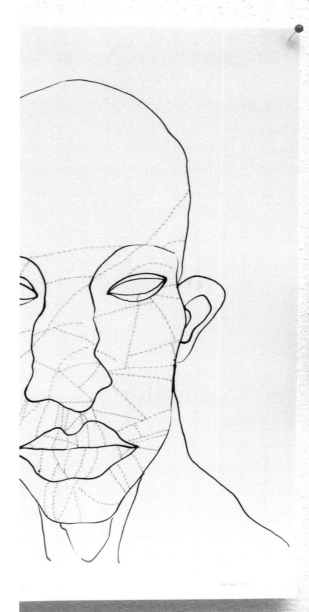

Autodidakt by Jesper
Waldersten

Mental Talk by Kalle
Mattsson

Most Tall Snake by Kalle
Mattsson

Monster by Geoff
McFetridge

Untitled by Saeko Takagi

Elephant by Hellovon

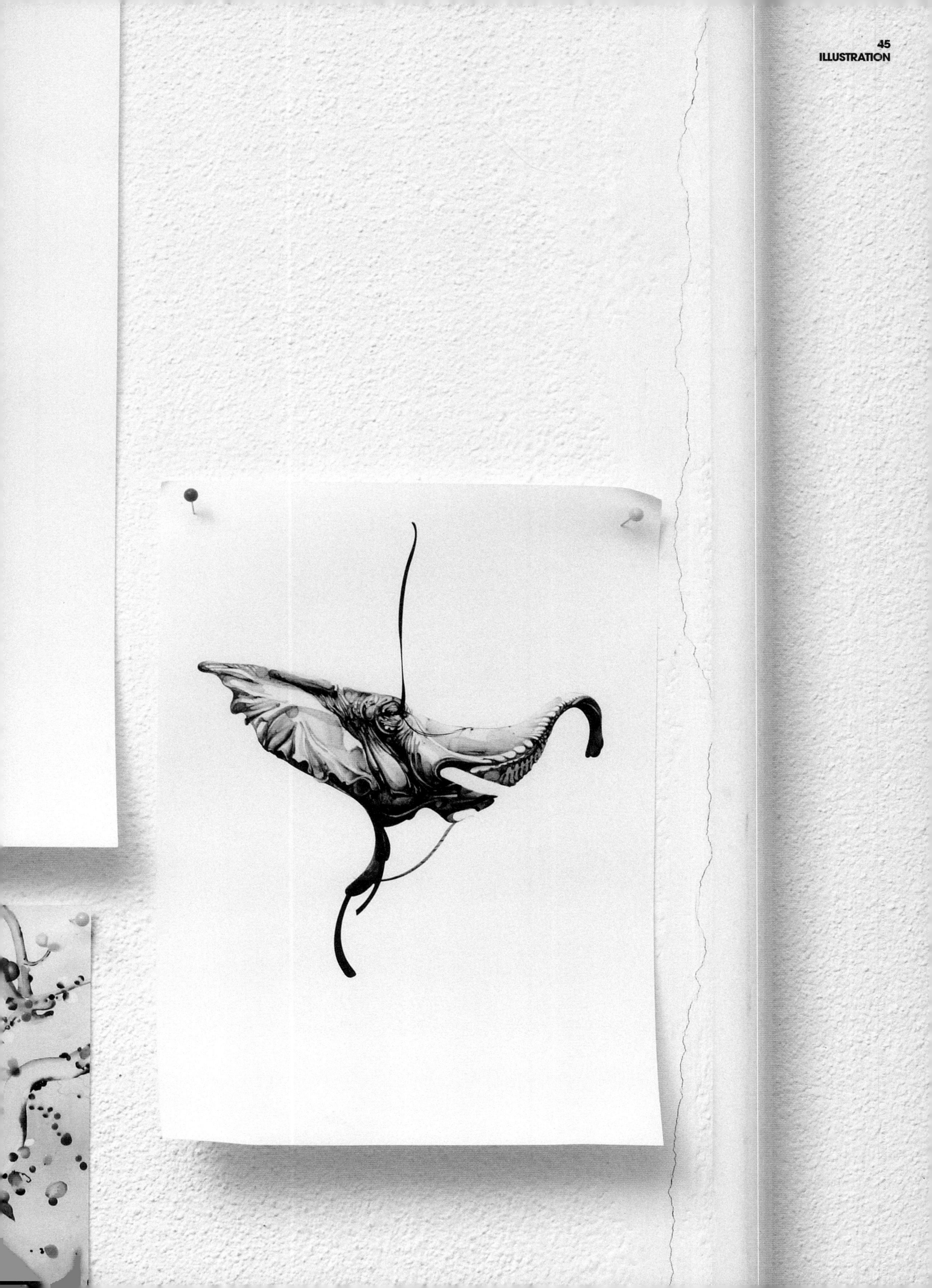

MARTIN KLIMAS
Falling guns

TIM GUTT
From the view-master reel
Between The Lines, 2006.

VIVIANE SASSEN
Untitled (Ghana 2007),
from the series Ultra Violet,
courtesy Motive Gallery
Amsterdam

PHOTOGRAPHY

JUERGEN TELLER

Juergen Teller has been shooting the Marc Jacobs campaigns for several years now and his work is consistently amazing. The pictures have created their own world with real people in real clothes in unmediated moments. It's very generous, which is the opposite of what fashion and fashion photography usually are. *(Jop van Bennekom)*

www.marcjacobs.com

JOËL TETTAMANTI
RACHEL THOMAS

This year I discovered these beautiful incidental landscapes and architectural observations. Otherwise I always like what Rachel Thomas produces, with whomever she collaborates. *(Joe Burrin)*

www.tettamanti.ch
www.bigactive.com

MARTIN KLIMAS

He keeps capturing little scenes at the exact moment I would most like to see them. Beautifully crafted (not-so-still) life. *(Kjell Ekhorn)*

www.martin-klimas.de

JOHANNES SCHWARTZ

Johannes Schwartz, whom we work with quite often (on publications like High Noon, High Nature, High Light and High Rise, and more recently on the exhibition Stair/Stare at Marres in Maastricht), has a book out, and it is an excellent introduction to his work. Published and designed by Willem van Zoetendaal, Das Prinzip (The Principle) carries a sharp and handsome selection of Schwartz's photographs.

What characterises Schwartz's work is his very precise, analytical, almost obsessively technical eye. What we find particularly interesting about Schwartz is his fascination with 'the object'; not only the photographed object, but also the exploration of the photographic image as an object in its own right. *(Experimental Jetset)*

www.saatchi-gallery.co.uk
www.vanzoetendaal.nl

MARTIN KLIMAS

His photographs are visual feasts, one and all. *(Jon Forss)*

www.martin-klimas.de

EMANUEL ALMBORG

What are people doing in his pictures and why? *(Martin Frostner)*

www.sakerna.se

TIM GUTT

I have been a fan of Tim Gutt's work for some time, but I think this year was a real breakthrough for him. His Jil Sander shoot for Dazed & Confused raised the bar for magazine fashion photography—and put the fashion brand's own advertising campaign in the shade. Gutt uses white space with the confidence of a photographer who knows he is right. So rather than feeling blank, or empty, the clear backgrounds hold the figures in space. Their intensity of colour, pace as a collection of images, and compositional poise ennoble the clothes, the models and the viewer. His Tall Fashion shoot for Kilimanjaro also has enormous impact, and the kind of tension that repays many subsequent viewings. *(William Hall)*

www.timgutt.com

TINY VICES

No one photographer, but Tim Barber's fantastic photography site Tiny Vices. The perfect antidote to the blandness of Flickr. *(Richard Hogg)*

www.tinyvices.com

FLICKR

I'm completely obsessed with Flickr, and am enjoying the mix of professional, hobbyist and amateur photography—seeing things in different ways. *(Corey Holms)*

www.flickr.com/photos/whinger/favorites/

VIVIANE SASSEN

(Ben Parker)

www.vivianesassen.com

PETER SUTHERLAND

I met Peter playing football in Chinatown. His football is patchy. His photography is inspirational. There is an unerring honesty to the images he captures. His work represents a composed allegory of the point-and-shoot hangover. I would recommend his books Coming Home, Game and

the latest publication on Power House called Buck Shots. *(Tom Phillips)*

www.petersutherland.net

CHRIS BROOKS

Best friend and now a CLM cohort, my top pick is and always will be Chris Brooks. *(Danny Sangra)*

www.iamchrisbrooks.com

CHARLOTT MARKUS

(Jens Schildt)

www.charlottmarkus.com

YELENA YEMCHUCK

I'm a big fan of Yelena Yemchuck at Art Dept. *(Becky Smith)*

www.art-dept.com/artists/yemchuk

NICK VEASEY

You should see the harsh industrial environment, the process, the danger, and the lengths Nick goes to, to create such beautiful, otherworldly images. *(StudioThomson)*

www.untitled.co.uk

RICHARD LEAROYD

Photographing the day. *(Charlie Thomas)*

www.richardlearoyd.com

SANDRA FREIJ

There is a lot going on with Sandra Freij's work. Something seems to be lurking below the surface of her images. They are always otherworldly in some way and very, very elegant. There is also a strong sense of narrative in her work that I am attracted to. We recently collaborated on a little trilogy of images and she was a joy to work with, very talented. The new Sarah Moon… *(Rachel Thomas)*

www.theannasuagency.com/website/index.htm

INEZ VAN LAMSVEERDE AND VINOODH MATADIN

Constantly pushing fashion photography comfortably with one foot in the arts and one in commerce. *(Erik Torstensson)*

www.artandcommerce.com

GILES REVELL

Consistently inventive and intelligent approach to anything he takes on. He has an astonishingly creative and relentlessly active mind. Shamelessly mimicked, ripped-off occasionally. *(Matt Willey)*

www.gilesrevell.com

EMANUEL ALMBORG
From the series Captured,
images taken in zoos
around New York, 2007

RICHARD LEAROYD
Orla Keeley, SS08

YELENA YEMCHUCK
From the series White
Russian for Japanese
Vogue, 2007

JOHANNES SCHWARTZ
From the series
Winkels, exhibited at Van
Zoetendaal Collections,
Amsterdam, 2007

OBS

LOS ANGELES   LAS VEGAS   PARIS
PEI   HONG KONG   SHANGHAI
RIYADH   DUBAI   KUWAIT CITY

MICHAEL STIPE PHOTOGRAPHED BY JUERGEN TELLER

JEURGEN TELLER
Michael Stipe for Marc
Jacobs 2007

PETER SUTHERLAND 1
Final Moth, from the series
Dirt Land

PETER SUTHERLAND 2
Smoke Face from the
series Dirt Land

CHRIS BROOKS
Still life, sunglasses in
local church, 2007

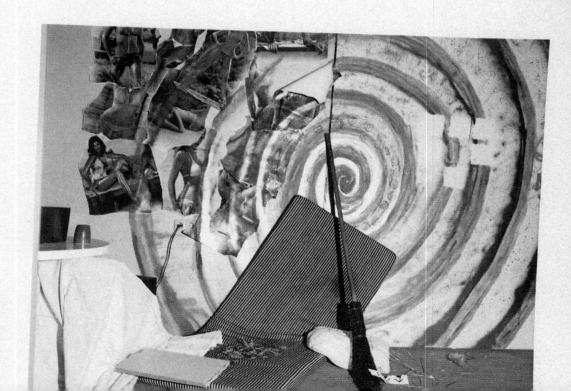

CHARLOTT MARKUS
From the series Pygmalion,
light box installation at
Gerrit Rietveld Academie,
Amsterdam 2007

MAGAZINES

ONENESS

Of course it is not the done thing to name my own magazines here, so I'll go for the Taiwanese magazine Oneness—which managed not only to copy Fantastic Man's design in detail but also the editorial contents of Re-Magazine at the same time. *(Jop van Bennekom)*

TYPOGRAPHY PAPERS, PUBLISHED BY THE DEPARTMENT OF TYPOGRAPHY & GRAPHIC COMMUNICATION AT THE UNIVERSITY OF READING

It's such a beautifully designed, interesting, well-written, non-hyped and intelligent graphic design publication. Calling it a magazine is maybe not even doing it justice. *(Sara De Bondt)*

www.hyphenpress.co.uk

FANTASTIC MAN

Another very slick Jop van Bennekom outing— elegant layouts, strong type, lovely paper stocks and a great, great name. Plus the content isn't bad either. *(Joe Burrin)*

www.fantasticmanmagazine.com

ARENA HOMME+ WINTER/SPRING 07/08

Such a nice surprise to see M/M Paris injecting some crazy French freshness into the classic men's fashion magazine. *(Kjell Ekhorn)*

www.arenamagazine.co.uk

THE SOUND PROJECTOR

We happened to be at Rough Trade in Soho on the last day that it was open, and acquired issue 15 of The Sound Projector. It's a music magazine so esoteric that it makes The Wire look like Smash Hits. Page after page obsessively filled with reviews organised in chronological order, featuring rather obscure bands (mostly of the noise and black metal variety) with colourful names such as 666majik999 and Solar Anus. Captured in the magazine is the promise of music as a slightly sinister, potentially dangerous force; a sensation that we haven't felt in a long time. The magazine is edited, designed and written by Ed Pinsent, who also happened to be involved in Escape, a really great British comic that was published in the Eighties. *(Experimental Jetset)*

www.thesoundprojector.com

IDEA

Japan's Idea magazine still reigns supreme. Last year there were wonderful Kazunari Hattori and Ed Fella specials. This year, Jan Tschichold, Otl Aicher and Wim Crouwel specials, one after the other. *(Jon Forss)*

www.idea-mag.com

HOMEWARD BOUND OR AN EXERCISE IN COLLECTING BEGINNINGS

A loose-leaf publication informed by a research fellowship at the British Library by Lizzie Ridout, this has amazing content inspired by ghosts of stockings and skull-stitched dresses. *(Martin Frostner)*

www.lizzieridout.com

DIGITAL CAMERA WORLD

Tips for amateur to hobbyist photographers, which I find fairly useful. *(Corey Holms)*

NEW SCIENTIST

One of the few magazines either of us buy with any regularity, New Scientist can always be relied upon to give new knowledge and inspiration. *(Hudson Powell)*

www.newscientist.com

HAMBURGER EYES

It doesn't get any better than Hamburger Eyes. This independently published epic comes out of San Francisco every couple of seasons. It is a photographic odyssey. Each issue is woven together from a patchwork of shooters. There are barely any words in it and it has the best name ever. I have hamburger eyes for Hamburger Eyes. *(Tom Phillips)*

www.burgerworldchronicles.com

CODE

I like the Dutch magazine CODE's freshness—it keeps me in touch with what's going on, on a 'younger' and street level. It also has a surprisingly calm layout, unlike a lot of other Dutch magazines, which are 'zo overdreven' (over the top) that you cannot tell the difference between the ads and the editorial. Designed simply and effectively by Toko. *(David Quay)*

www.code-mag.nl

SELF SERVICE 26—OVERLY CHLOE

I can't choose a new magazine because they are all starting to look the same. *(Danny Sangra)*

www.selfservicemagazine.com

FANTASTIC MAN

For an alternative to my own, I like Fantastic Man… it's truly fantastic. *(Becky Smith)*

www.fantasticmanmagazine.com

ROULEUR

A cycling magazine of exquisite photography and writing created to celebrate the drama and beauty of road racing. *(StudioThomson)*

www.rouleur.co.uk

ARCHITECTURAL DIGEST, ITALIAN AND SPANISH EDITIONS, CONDÉ NAST PUBLICATIONS

I occasionally pick up either of these versions of AD magazine. It's a through-the-keyhole glimpse into a variety of aesthetic characters (all wealthy). It throws up all sorts of styles, often not entirely to my liking. However, being continental, they embrace a mix of classic and contemporary with true panache. *(Charlie Thomas)*

www.architecturaldigest.com

MAN ABOUT TOWN

I have to say our own Man About Town. It was a big deal for us to get the chance not only to art-direct but to be the editorial directors for a men's fashion magazine this year. *(Erik Torstensson)*

www.manabouttownonline.com

ROGER

ROGER magazine: Design People Questions is the only contemporary academic tome that I have been able to wrap my brain around this year, in periods of self-improvement. *(Robert Urquhart)*

www.roger.kisd.de

IDEA

If we are talking about a visually pleasing magazine, rather than a magazine that has wonderful written content (these shouldn't necessarily be mutually exclusive), then Idea #323: Wim Crouwel is very good. *(Matt Willey)*

www.idea-mag.com

TATE ETC.

The magazine published by the Tate Gallery always impresses us. It completely reflects the ability of the Tate to frame its content in both a popular and intelligent way, to be in-depth in a non-elitist way, and it also looks great. *(YES Studio)*

www.tate.org.uk/tateetc

Hamburger Eyes,
Issue 008

Homeward Bound
by Lizzie Ridout

Rouleur, Issue three

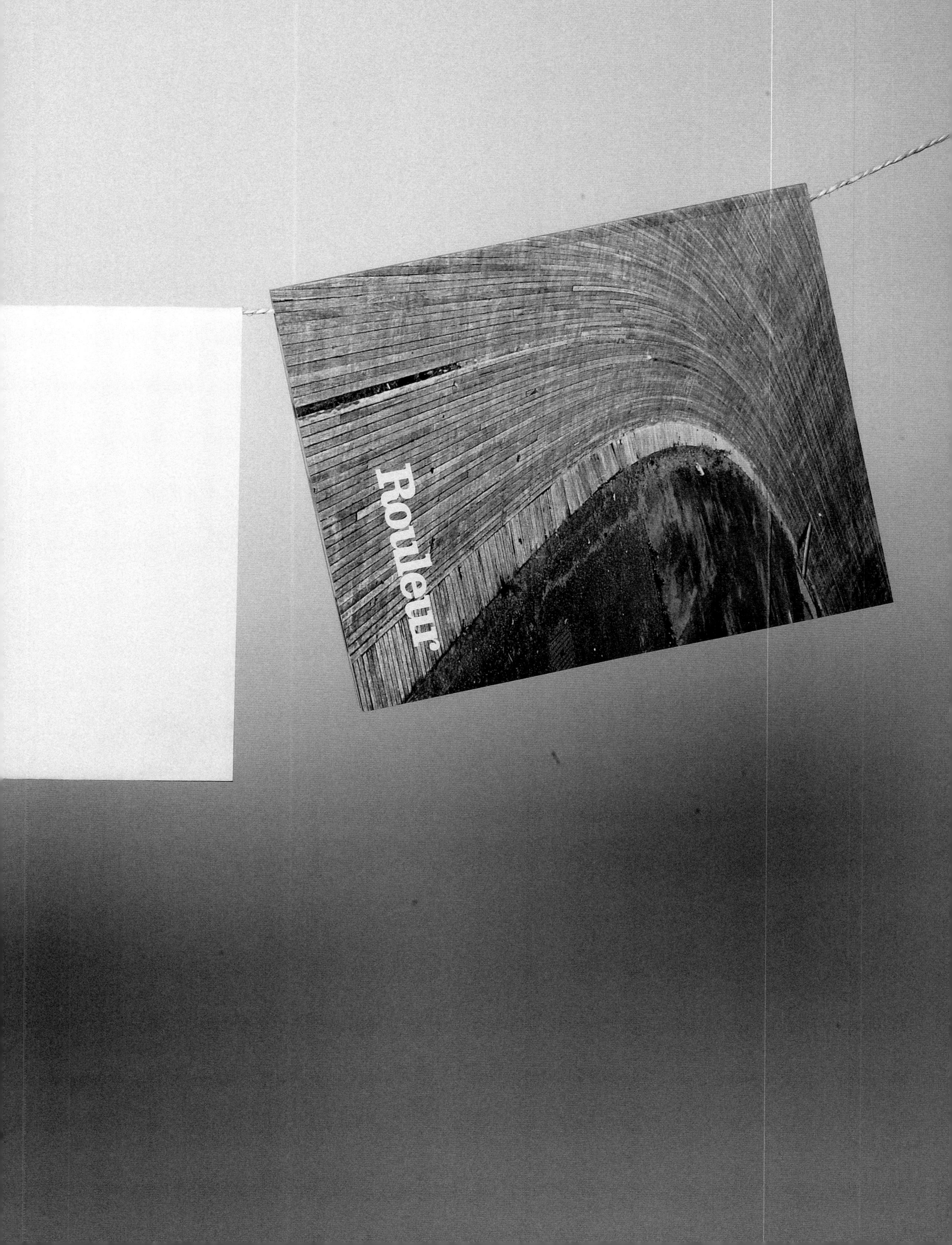
Rouleur

Fantastic Man, Issue 6:
Autumn Winter 2007-8

Code, Issue 8, Autumn
Winter, 2007

Tate Etc, Issue 11, Autumn
2007

The Little Know It All: Common Sense for Designers by Robert Klanten

Taking the Matter into Common Hands

Eat London by Terence Conran, Peter Prescott and Lisa Linder

The Zeeland Tapestries by Katie Heyning

Bob Richardson by Terry Richardson

Le Corbusier—The Art of Architecture by Stanislaus von Moos, Arthur Rüegg, Alexander von Vegesack and Mateo Kries

BOB RICHARDSON

BOOKS

THE ECHO CHAMBER BY LUKE WILLIAMS PUBLISHED BY HAMISH HAMILTON

A fantastic piece of literary fiction on auditive memory, Empire, the history of map-making, colonialism and growing up written by a young Scottish writer called Luke Williams. *(Sara De Bondt)*

www.penguin.co.uk

KARA WALKER: MY COMPLEMENT, MY ENEMY... BY THOMAS MCEVILLEY AND PHILIPPE VERGNE, PUBLISHED BY WALKER ARTS CENTRE

The catalogue for Kara Walker's exhibition at the Walker Art Center in Minneapolis is scarily well designed. With its shades of brown ink, paper stocks and referential choice of typefaces Kara Walker simply became a graphic style in it- (or her-) self. *(Jop van Bennekom)*

www.walkerart.org

CARSTEN NICOLAI—STATIC FADES, EDITED BY DOROTHEA STRAUSS, PUBLISHED BY JRPIRINGIER

Any one of the various books I picked up from the publisher JRPIRingier—catalogues for Mathieu Mercier or Carsten Nicolai to highlight just a few. *(Joe Burrin)*

www.jrp-ringier.com

CHARLEY HARPER: AN ILLUSTRATED LIFE BY TODD OLDHAM, PUBLISHED BY AMMO BOOKS

This is the one I want for Christmas. *(Kjell Ekhorn)*

www.ammobooks.com

IN GIRUM IMUS NOCTE ET CONSUMIMUR IGNI— THE SITUATIONIST INTERNATIONAL (1957—72), PUBLISHED BY JRPIRINGIER

Casually designed by a Swiss named Marie Lusa, and published on the occasion of an exhibition on the Situationist International, this book is a rich and interesting document. Whereas most other books on the subject focus mainly on the textual side of the Situationists and neglect the form in which these texts originally appeared, it shows the Situationist movement in all its ephemeral glory, through collages, postcards, sketches, maps, manifestos and photographs. *(Experimental Jetset)*

www.jrp-ringier.com

CHARLEY HARPER: AN ILLUSTRATED LIFE BY TODD OLDHAM, PUBLISHED BY AMMO BOOKS

I'm going to champion the Charlie Harper book because his work looks as fresh and contemporary as that of any vector-based illustrator of today. *(Jon Forss)*

www.ammobooks.com

DIE SCHÖNSTEN SCHWEIZER BÜCHER 2006, PUBLISHED BY BUNDESAMT FÜR KULTUR, BERN

I know that the catalogue/book for the Die Schönsten Schweizer Bücher (The Most Beautiful Swiss Books) has been around for some years but I think the designers Laurent Benner and Jon Hares deserve severe respect for inventing the ultimate solution in how to present nice books in print. *(Martin Frostner)*

www.bak.admin.ch

TORD BOONTJE BY MARTINA MARGETTS, PUBLISHED BY RIZZOLI INTERNATIONAL

Designed by Graphic Thought Facility *(Ben Parker)*

www.rizzoliusa.com

THE ZEELAND TAPESTRIES BY KATIE HEYNING, PUBLISHED BY ZEEUWS MUSEUM

During of the Eighty Years' War of Dutch independence against the Spanish, Middelburg celebrated its victory by weaving a series of huge tapestries detailing every important event in the war. This book is information-heavy but still full of the interesting design ideas that only Dutch designers seem to get away with. *(David Quay)*

www.hansgremmen.nl

THE LITTLE KNOW IT ALL: COMMON SENSE FOR DESIGNERS BY ROBERT KLANTEN, PUBLISHED BY DGV

Pretty geeky but the only newly published book I bought this year. *(Danny Sangra)*

www.die-gestalten.de

SCOTT PILGRIM GETS IT TOGETHER BY BRYAN O'MALLEY, PUBLISHED BY ONI PRESS

It isn't even out yet but I am very excited about it. *(Jens Schildt)*

www.onipress.com

NY JS DB 62 BY MARTIN HARRISON, PUBLISHED BY STEIDL

This book is based on a shoot in New York for Vogue magazine with David Bailey and Jean Shrimpton. There was no hairdresser or make-up artist on the shoot, Jean did her own. Bailey and Shrimpton broke new ground for fashion. Fashion was no longer static and stiff, posed in the studio, it became something that was relevant and current. *(Becky Smith)*

www.steidlville.com

TAKING THE MATTER INTO COMMON HANDS: CONTEMPORARY ART AND COLLABORATIVE PRACTICES, EDITED BY JOHANNA BILLING, MARIA LIND AND LARS NILSSON, PUBLISHED BY BLACK-DOG PUBLISHING.

(Frauke Stegman)

www.blackdogonline.com

LE CORBUSIER—THE ART OF ARCHITECTURE BY STANISLAUS VON MOOS, ALEXANDER VON VEGESACK, ARTHUR RÜEGG AND MATEO KRIES, PUBLISHED BY THE VITRA DESIGN MUSEUM

An intriguing flick through the sketchbooks and personal artifacts that influenced his architecture and furniture. *(StudioThomson)*

www.design-museum.de

KENNETH MARTIN & MARY MARTIN: CONSTRUCTED WORKS, PUBLISHED BY CAMDEN ARTS CENTRE

Designed by Fraser Muggeridge Studio *(Charlie Thomas)*

camdenartscenter.org

COME ALIVE! THE SPIRITED ART OF SISTER CORITA BY JULIE AULT, PUBLISHED BY FOUR CORNERS

My introduction to Sister Corita came via a piece in Frieze about ten years ago. I was shocked and intrigued by the idea of a nun making Pop Art. Then I stumbled on this book completely by chance—it was like having a revelation. It is a great book with lots of reproductions, as well as documentation of her and the order of nuns she belonged to creating fantastic happenings. *(Rachel Thomas)*

www.fourcornersbooks.com

BOB RICHARDSON BY TERRY RICHARDSON, PUBLISHED BY DAMIANI

Bob Richardson sired Terry and was an even more inspiring photographer. *(Erik Torstensson)*

www.damianieditore.it

EAT LONDON BY TERENCE CONRAN, PETER PRESCOTT AND LISA LINDER, PUBLISHED BY CONRAN OCTOPUS

I got a lot of pleasure from Eat London, designed by Untitled. It's so simple and so well thought out. The cover, which folds out to show a map of London highlighting all the featured places to eat, is brilliant. *(Matt Willey)*

www.conran.co.uk

AUTOS BY BERNARD FUCHS, PUBLISHED BY KOENIG BOOKS LONDON

While cycling, Bernhard Fuchs took pictures of passenger cars, trucks and buses which were just left standing around, their owners absent. In his words: "The cars in the landscape had an impact on me, similar to the impact of actors on a stage, and since then I began to collect their wit and tragedy." *(YES Studio)*

www.koenigbooks.co.uk

WA

DÉPASEMENT DE LART

The End of
Uncle Tom
and the
Grand
Allegorical
Tableau of
Eva in
Heaven

KENNETH MARTIN & MARY MARTIN:
CONSTRUCTED WORKS

FORD TIMES

september 1954

Autos by Bernard Fuchs

Charley Harper: An
illustrated Life
by Todd Oldham

Prism #1 by Stateless,
12-inch single, designed
by Non-Format

MUSIC PACKAGING

RUSHUP EDGE BY THE TUSS, REPHLEX

Is it a shame that music—or actually MP3s—comes without packaging these days? I personally never got over the fact that the size of CDs doesn't have that appeal of the LPs, the 12-inches—or even the 7-inches—I grew up with. The design of The Tuss's CD Rushup Edge is simply a blank CD in an unprinted standard jewel box with a little card stuck into it. It looks like a mistake. I like it. *(Jop van Bennekom)*

www.roughtrade.com

WILL HOLDER'S DID YOU KISS THE FOOT THAT KICKED YOU? LEAFLET FOR ARTIST RUTH EWAN.

It's not strictly packaging any music, but it goes with the recording of a folk song originally written by Ewan MacColl. I love its use of paper, colour, fonts and format. It's really simple and just the way it should be. *(Sara De Bondt)*

MOOG ACID

I particularly like Dan McPharlin's cardboard models Non-Format have used for Moog Acid: Jacques Perry/Luke Vibert or any of their Lo Alternative Frequencies artwork—the Von one was nice. *(Joe Burrin)*

ULTRALYD—CONDITIONS FOR A PIECE OF MUSIC, RUNE GRAMMOFON

Difficult one this year as I have spent too much time in the studio… I would very much like a copy of Ultralyd: Conditions for a Piece of Music—the limited-edition LP which temptingly is announced with 'different colours on the front' on Rune Grammofon's website. I haven't seen it in the flesh so I shouldn't vote for it—but I guess I have. *(Kjell Ekhorn)*

GHOST BOX

The movement that we find most interesting in contemporary art and design is the tendency among a small group of designers and artists to try to explore new possible interpretations of modernism. A good example of this can be found in the graphic design of Julian House, who offers a very personal and highly idiosyncratic perspective on modernism. He looks at historical modernism from an occult viewpoint, trying to explore the relationship between the paranormal and the pop-cultural. This perspective is most visible in the CD sleeves he designs for his own label, Ghost Box. 2007 saw the release of two Ghost Box CDs, We Are All Pan's People and The Seance at Hobs Lane. Both CD sleeves are perfect examples of JH's specific blend of 'magickal' modernism, a place where the Hammer House of Horror meets the Bauhaus. *(Experimental Jetset)*

www.ghostbox.co.uk/

SMALLTOWN SUPERJAZZ HEALTHY BOY

Kim Hiorthøy's sleeves for Smalltown Superjazz look great. In particular Mats Gustafsson/Paal Nilssen-Love's Slatter, Original Silence's First Original Silence album and the Mats Gustafsson & Yoshimi album Words on the Floor. Grandpeople's packaging for the Healthy Boy label—their work has never been stronger and the illustrative work they are creating for this label looks amazing. Can't wait to see more. *(Jon Forss)*

MIRRORED BY BATTLES, WARP

I'm going to be boring and say the Battles record, even though I find the music tiresome. It's a great bit of art direction and I like looking at all the stuff in it. *(Richard Hogg)*

www.bttls.com
www.timothysaccenti.com

SIMPLE SOUNDS, SIMPLE RECORDS

I've always been interested in work that shows objects in places they don't belong. It somehow speaks to me, that moment of discovery that something isn't right, although initially it looks like everything is normal. I wonder about finding something like that on a walk—I think if I found an Andy Goldsworthy piece in the forest it would scare me. *(Corey Holms)*

www.wearebuild.com/projects/simple-sounds

GENGHIS TRON—DEAD MOUNTAIN MOUTH, CRUCIAL BLAST

The Dead Mountain Mouth LP packaging was shot and designed by OSK design. The cover image has an intrigue similar to a Where's Wally? kid's book or symbolist painting, and is packed with detail to draw you in. *(Hudson Powell)*

www.oskdesign.com/genghis1

PEOPLE I ADORE—PTTRNS, URSA MINOR MUSIK

Seven-inch vinyl record from the German band PTTRNS called People I Adore, designed by One-DayNation. *(Jens Schildt)*

www.onedaynation.com

STAND YOUR GROUND BY LITTLE BARRIE, GENUINE.

The design is based around a lovely piece of typography that appears on a poster and CD within, and on the cover, foiled in gold. *(StudioThomson)*

STATELESS

The record sleeves that Non-Format did for Stateless were fantastic. What Non-Format do with type is, on occasion, simply brilliant. But the truth is I don't own these records and, if Dylan or Waits or Laurie Anderson or Lucinda Williams or Gillian Welch or Mazzy Star (I could go on) produced a great album tomorrow, I'd buy it regardless of the front cover or the packaging. *(Matt Willey)*

www.statelessonline.co.uk
www.non-format.com/

RADIOHEAD—IN RAINBOWS

Disappointingly, nothing has especially caught our eye this year. However, we did respect the way that Radiohead went about distributing and publicising their new album. *(YES Studio)*

www.inrainbows.com

Mirrored by Battles, designed by Dave Konopka, photography by Timothy Saccenti

Moog Acid by Jean Jaques Perrey and Luke Vibert, sleeve notes and 12-inch double LP featuring models and photography by Dan McPharlin

People I Adore by PTTRNS, 7-inch single, designed by OneDayNation

(F) "BIG HANDS"
BIG HANDS ON THE TABLE AND I CAN'T SEE
TO PUT AWAY MY SWORDS HAS BEEN MY DEFEAT
FENCE ME IN I'VE CALLED FOR WIRE
AND I READ THE BOOKS THAT SPELL SURVIVING
THE GROUND'S THE CEILING
    BIG HANDS ARE PERMANENT
    GOLD MINES ARE NEVER MEANT
SINGING THE SERMON ALL NIGHT ON THE SHORE
FOR BIG HANDS AND NEW WAVE HEARTS
FOR BIG HANDS AND THE WAVE OF THE YOUNG
SINGING THE SERMON ALL NIGHT FROM THE ROOFTOPS
IT'S THE LAST TIME LOVERS AND TRAITORS PREVAIL
FOR THOUSAND YEARS OF HUSTLING
THE CARAVAN MAGIC IS SO PASSÉ
    BIG HANDS ARE PERMANENT
    GOLD MINES ARE NEVER MEANT
SAY IT ALL IT'S A SILENCE THAT KEEPS ON LASTING

    (A) "IDLE EYES, SORE CITY"
HE FLOATS — SHE FLOATS
MESSAGES DEFLATE — PATTERNS DECODE
    ON THE FENCES OF THE CHURCHYARDS
    BETWEEN THE PILLOWS OF THE HOSPITAL BEDS
    DEAD SIGNS WALKING ON DEAD SIGNS WALKING
    ON DEAD SIGNS WALKING ON THIS
YOU'RE SO GOOD
IN THE CHAMBERS
YOUR COLLECTION'S THE TALK OF THE TOWN
STRIPPED DOWN WHEN THE MATADOR SETS FOOT
CAN'T TELL THE CENTER OF TIME
DEAD SIGNS IN THE HOSPITAL THEY FLOAT
ON THE BODIES OF THE TALK OF THE TOWN

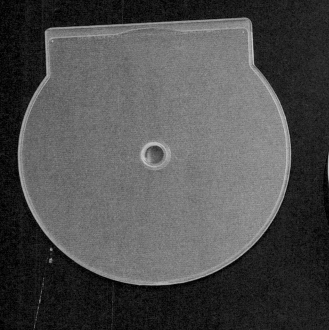

DVD-R 1-16x

he Floor by Mats
and Yoshimi,
designed by Kim

e by The Tuss
ith sticker

For A Piece
Ultralyd, CD
gned by Kim

nds by Will .
um, designed

Times Roman by Stanley Morison

TYPEFACES

CLASSICS

I don't really keep track of new type designs since I only use five different classic typefaces. They do the trick just fine. *(Jop van Bennekom)*

OFFENBACH

Annette Lux's digitised version of Rudolf Koch's Offenbach—I hope she finishes it this year, because it's gorgeous and I'm dying to use it. It looks like it was drawn with a quill pen, but takes it beyond a simple 'calligraphic' feel into something really elegant and well thought through.
(Sara De Bondt)
www.polylux.co.uk

INDEX BOLD/STYMIE HAIRLINE

The custom cut of Stymie Hairline that I worked on earlier this year. Otherwise Index Bold. *(Joe Burrin)*
www.optimo.ch

HERMES

Typeface of the year, again. *(Kjell Ekhorn)*
www.optimo.ch

BP NEUTRAL

2007 was the year that Kai Bernau's typeface Neutral was finally made commercially available. Originally a graduation project from 2005, Neutral is an interesting typeface as it tries to combine two seemingly opposing qualities: neutrality and self-referentiality. In other words, Neutral is a typeface that is neutral, but also makes a statement about neutrality. It's a difficult position, some would say a paradoxical one. Can something be neutral while simultaneously keeping a critical distance from its own neutrality? This is almost an existential problem: can a person truly be him/herself, while being fully aware of being him/herself? Can you look at yourself, through your own eyes? You would need an out-of-body experience to achieve that. Which describes exactly what Neutral is: a typeface having an out-of-body experience.
(Experimental Jetset)
http://www.letterlabor.de
http://www.bpfoundry.com

HERMES/TYP1451A & B

For me this year has been all about creating our own typefaces, whether that's applying the 'hand job' method or keeping things crisp with vectors. But I've lost count of the number of times I've used either Optimo's Hermes or Lineto's Typ1451A & B, which are both really great utilitarian typefaces.
(Jon Forss)
www.optimo.ch
www.lineto.com

UNIVERS, FOLIO, RECTA AND MERCATOR

Since Helvetica is the world's official fifty-year old celebrity I think it would be nice to sing a song for the twins born in the same year: Univers, Folio, Recta and Mercator. *(Martin Frostner)*

TIMES ROMAN

There has been much talk of the fiftieth anniversary of Helvetica this year, but almost nothing in celebration of Times Roman, which is seventy-five. Its current ubiquity is partly due to its having been standard issue with all computers since the early 1990s. Unfortunately Microsoft Word makes it look terrible because the spacing is so poor, but properly spaced Times Roman looks great. When I redesigned our letterhead in 2003, I decided to use Times Roman because its ubiquity makes it invisible, and because it's almost never seen in a design environment. I wanted to show that Times Roman is a brilliant and underappreciated font.
(William Hall)

BURGUES SCRIPT

Burgues Script by Alejandro Paul—crazy-ass OpenType goodness. With a massive substitution library and stylistic alternatives, you can pretty much do anything you want. *(Corey Holms)*
www.veer.com

OPTIMA

We've been trying to bring about a renaissance of humanist and flare serif fonts recently. Their subtle curves have been overlooked for too long.
(Hudson Powell)
www.linotype.com

NEW CENTURY SCHOOLBOOK

(Ben Parker)

DIDOT

I was just introduced to Didot by an up-and-coming typographer known as 'The Fist'. I like it. It's nice. I will be using it. I promised The Fist I would not tell anyone else about it. You know how it goes. *(Tom Phillips)*

TYPEFACE FOR DIE HALLEN HAARLEM

This is not great type design but as an idea it's perfect. It holds the whole identity of this very small art gallery in Haarlem together simply and effectively. *(David Quay)*
www.cobbenhagenhendriksen.nl

HAND DRAWN

Anything hand-scribbled in black felt tip on a band flyer this year. *(Danny Sangra)*

MIDO AND NUMBER 9

Mido by Eva Grinder and Number 9 by Ian Brown. *(Jens Schildt)*
www.midofont.se
www.ianswork.net

LULA

Can I pick my own Lula typeface? See current issue five throughout. Unique and it has so much mileage and possibilities for the future.
(Becky Smith)

LE CORBUSIER

A quintessentially French stencil font based on his design notations and cataloguing system.
(Studio Thomson)
www.lineto.com/

GOTHAM

Gotham. Medium and Bold, only in uppercase.
(Erik Torstensson)
www.typography.com

ROLETTA

Roletta. It's a new font by Andrea Tinnes which I've just used for a magazine redesign. It works really well as a text font. It's this week's favourite… last week it was Lutz Headline. *(Matt Willey)*
http://www.typecuts.com

LINETO

We're not going to single out one typeface here, but instead tip our hats to the continuing greatness of type foundry Lineto. Like a great independent label, but for type. *(YES Studio)*
www.lineto.com

Lula by Becky Smith

Burgues Script by Alejandro Paul

Didot by Firmin Didot

S4C by Lineto
Roletta Serif by Annette Lux

Tidying up.

TYPEFACE APPENDIX

Mido Medium
Ebenezer unexpectedly bagged two tranquil aardvarks with his jiffy vacuum cleaner.
abcdefghijklmnopqrstuvwxyz
ABCDEFGHIJKLMNOPQRSTUVWXYZ
1234567890
..,.:;«»&!?@˚/ §{}ΩΣ

Hermes Sans
Pack my box with five dozen liquor jugs.
abcdefghijklmnopqrstuvwxyz
ABCDEFGHIJKLMNOPQRSTUVWXYZ
1234567890
.,.:;'"«»ß&!?£@%^*+="""

Roletta Serif
Jaded zombies acted quaintly but kept driving their oxen forward.
abcdefghijklmnopqrstuvwxyz
ABCDEFGHIJKLMNOPQRSTUVWXYZ
1234567890
.,.:;'"«»ß&!?£@%^*+=""<>\/|§±[]{}Ω®†¡Σ

Burgues Script
Fred specialized in the job of making very quaint wax toys.
abcdefghijklmnopqrstuvwxyz
ABCDEFGHIJKLMNOPQRSTUVWXYZ
1234567890
.,.:;'"«»ß&!?£@%^*+=""<>\/|§±[]{}Ω

Times Roman
Amazingly few discotheques provide jukeboxes.
abcdefghijklmnopqrstuvwxyz
ABCDEFGHIJKLMNOPQRSTUVWXYZ
1234567890
.,.:;'"«» ß&!?£@%^*+=""<>\/|§±[]{}Ω®†¡Σ

Didot
Whenever the black fox jumped the squirrel gazed suspiciously.
abcdefghijklmnopqrstuvwxyz
ABCDEFGHIJKLMNOPQRSTUVWXYZ
1234567890
.,.:;'" «»ß&!?£@%^*+= ""<>\/|§±[]{}Ω®†¡Σ

Lula Decorated
By Jove, my quick study of lexicography won a prize!
abcdefghijklmnopqrstuvwxyz
ABCDEFGHIJKLMNOPQRSTUVWXYZ
123456789
.,.:;'"«»SS&!? £@%^ *+=""<>/|§±[]{}Ω®†¡Σ

NUMBER 9
QUIT BEER VOWS DIZZY, PUKING, MICHAEL J. FOX.
abcdefghijklmnopqrstuvwxyz
ABCDEFGHIJKLMNOPQRSTUVWXYZ
1234567890
.,.:;'"«»ß&!?£@%^*+=""<>V|§±[]{}Ω®†

Folio
Six big devils from Japan quickly forgot how to waltz.
abcdefghijklmnopqrstuvwxyz
ABCDEFGHIJKLMNOPQRSTUVWXYZ
1234567890
.,.:;'"«»ß&!?£@%^*+=""<>\/|§±[]{}Ω®

Le Corbusier
Playing jazz vibe chords quickly excites my wife
abcdefghijklmnopqrstuvwxyz
ABCDEFGHIJKLMNOPQRSTUVWXYZ
1234567890
.,.:;'"«»ß&!?£@%^*+=""<>\/|§±[]{}®

S 4 C sans
Jackdaws love my big sphinx of quartz.
abcdefghijklmnopqrstuvwxyz
ABCDEFGHIJKLMNOPQRSTUVWXYZ
1234567890
.,.:;'"«»ß&!?£@%^*+=""<>\/|§±[]{}

The following typefaces were omitted from the appendix (either for reasons beyond our control, or simply because they didn't have numbers and special characters): BP Neutral, Gotham, Typeface for Die Hallen Haarlem, Index Bold, Mercator, New Century Schoolbook, Optima, Offenbach, Recta, Stymie Hairline and Univers.

Please also note that Lineto's LLTyp1451 typeface is shown here as S4C sans. It was adopted by the Welsh TV channel S4C as it's corporate font and is largely the same as LLTyp1451— but contains some subtle adaptation for the Welsh language.

49

EXHIBITIONS

KENNETH MARTIN AND MARY MARTIN: CONSTRUCTED WORKS, CAMDEN ARTS CENTRE

Their work still looks incredibly fresh and inspiring today. It makes me want to make things. *(Sara De Bondt)*

www.camdenartscentre.org

SEDUCED: ART AND SEX FROM ANTIQUITY TO NOW, BARBICAN GALLERY

This is tough but I'd recommend something fresh in my mind—Art and Sex from Antiquity to Now at the Barbican. *(Joe Burrin)*

www.barbican.org.uk/seduced.htm

LUIGI COLANI: TRANSLATING NATURE, DESIGN MUSEUM

Retro-futuristic dreams of the highest order. Took me right back to a time when the future was going to be ultra-exciting and very well designed. *(Kjell Ekhorn)*

www.designmuseum.org

HELIO OITICICA, TATE MODERN

We had seen some of Helio Oiticica's work before but to see such a large amount together, for the first time, certainly made a big impression on us. The exhibition showed how he took geometric art to the next level without betraying it. Oiticica's art is an inspiring example of how autonomy and engagement can be synthesised in a completely natural way. *(Experimental Jetset)*

www.tate.org.uk/modern/exhibitions/heliooiticica

WIM CROUWEL, D&AD LECTURE

Still as passionate about design as he must have been when he started his career all those decades ago. A true inspiration. *(Jon Forss)*

www.dandad.org

MARTINO GAMPER 100 CHAIRS IN 100 DAYS

Cast-off chairs, bicycle saddles and table legs, all collated, morphed, screwed and glued together to form 100 chairs, each one unique. Some are clumsy, some are ugly, others are beautiful. As a collection they have an incredible energy, something between a freak show, a zoo and shopping at Selfridges. *(William Hall)*

www.gampermartino.com

HENRY MOORE AT KEW

Can't wait to go back on a Wednesday morning in the middle of winter when there are no kids crawling all over them. *(Richard Hogg)*

www.kew.org/henry-moore

TYPECON 07

This event wasn't filled with all the usual hipsters and design-scene people, but much more with geeky, down-to-earth workaday designers. I learned more during the mealtime conversations than any of the lectures—a great sense of community. *(Corey Holms)*

www.typecon.com

COMIC ABSTRACTION, MOMA, NEW YORK

This exhibition bridges the gap between low brow and fine art and although the show is all based around abstraction there is a strong minimalist undertone to the work. *(Ben Parker)*

www.moma.org

ART OF THE PSYCHEDELIC ERA AT THE WHITNEY, NEW YORK

I wish it was the Sixties. I wish I could be happy. When you see this exhibition you realise that it probably was that good–I wasn't there but it looked like a right laugh from where I was standing in the Whitney. *(Tom Phillips)*

www.whitney.org

KHATT, KUFI AND KAFFIYA

A fantastic one-day conference with a cultural exchange of ideas and presentations from both Arabic and Dutch designers. *(David Quay)*

www.mediamatic.net/attachment-18361-en.html

THE TOMB OF ESTEBAN DORADO, EXHIBIT GALLERY

My show. *(Danny Sangra)*

www.exhibit-goldenlane.com

WHEN HELL FREEZES OVER BY MONICA TORMELL AT GALERIE VAN GELDER (AMSTERDAM)

Available1 at Gallery Plan B and any of the shows by Roky Erickson would also have been great. But I missed them. *(Jens Schildt)*

www.monicatormell.nl

ANNIE MORRIS, ALLSOPP CONTEMPORARY

(Becky Smith)

www.allsoppcontemporary.com

MARTINO GAMPER'S 100 CHAIRS IN 100 DAYS

Specifically the book launch at 5 Cromwell Place, 12 October 2007, with Bloodmusic playing. *(Frauke Stegmann)*

www.gampermartino.com
www.myspace.com/singasongfighter

TRASH LUXE, LIBERTY

An inspiring showcase found objects and cheap materials transformed into works of beauty and interest. *(StudioThomson)*

www.trashluxe.com

KENNETH MARTIN AND MARY MARTIN: CONSTRUCTED WORKS, CAMDEN ARTS CENTRE

A survey of the lifework of two artists who complemented each other perfectly. It felt as fresh and relevant now as it must have done forty years ago. *(Charlie Thomas)*

www.camdenartscentre.org
www.dlwp.com/

MOZART DANCES: MARK MORRIS DANCE GROUP AT BARBICAN

Contemporary choreography put to a familiar classical score with scenic painting by Howard Hodgkin. Totally enthralling in its simplicity albeit complexity. Genius… *(Charlie Thomas)*

www.mmdg.org

SPEED OF LIFE: MIKAEL JANSSON, KULTURHUSET STOCKHOLM

World-class prints, great lighting, truly amazing colours, and Formula 1 made into art by fashion photographer Mikael Jansson. Don't miss the beautiful book. *(Erik Torstensson)*

www.kulturhuset.stockholm.se

KAREN KILIMNIK, SERPENTINE GALLERY

I am totally fascinated by this woman's work. She's like a demented little girl who never grew up, obsessively looking in at a world she can never be part of. Instead she creates a relationship with it through making stuff and in the process she invents things, get things wrong, misinterprets and ends up creating a really potent and moving response to our culture. *(Rachel Thomas)*

www.serpentinegallery.org

DESIGN EVENT 07 (NEWCASTLE AND VARIOUS VENUES IN THE NORTH-EAST)

For pulling off a coherent mini-design festival. *(Robert Urquhart)*

www.design-event.co.uk

CHRISTOPH BÜCHEL, HAUSER & WIRTH

Abandoned factory spaces, a makeshift hotel, secret underground rooms and a half-excavated mammoth–this was one of the most ambitious large-scale exhibitions we've seen. *(YES Studio)*

www.hauserwirth.com/exhibitions

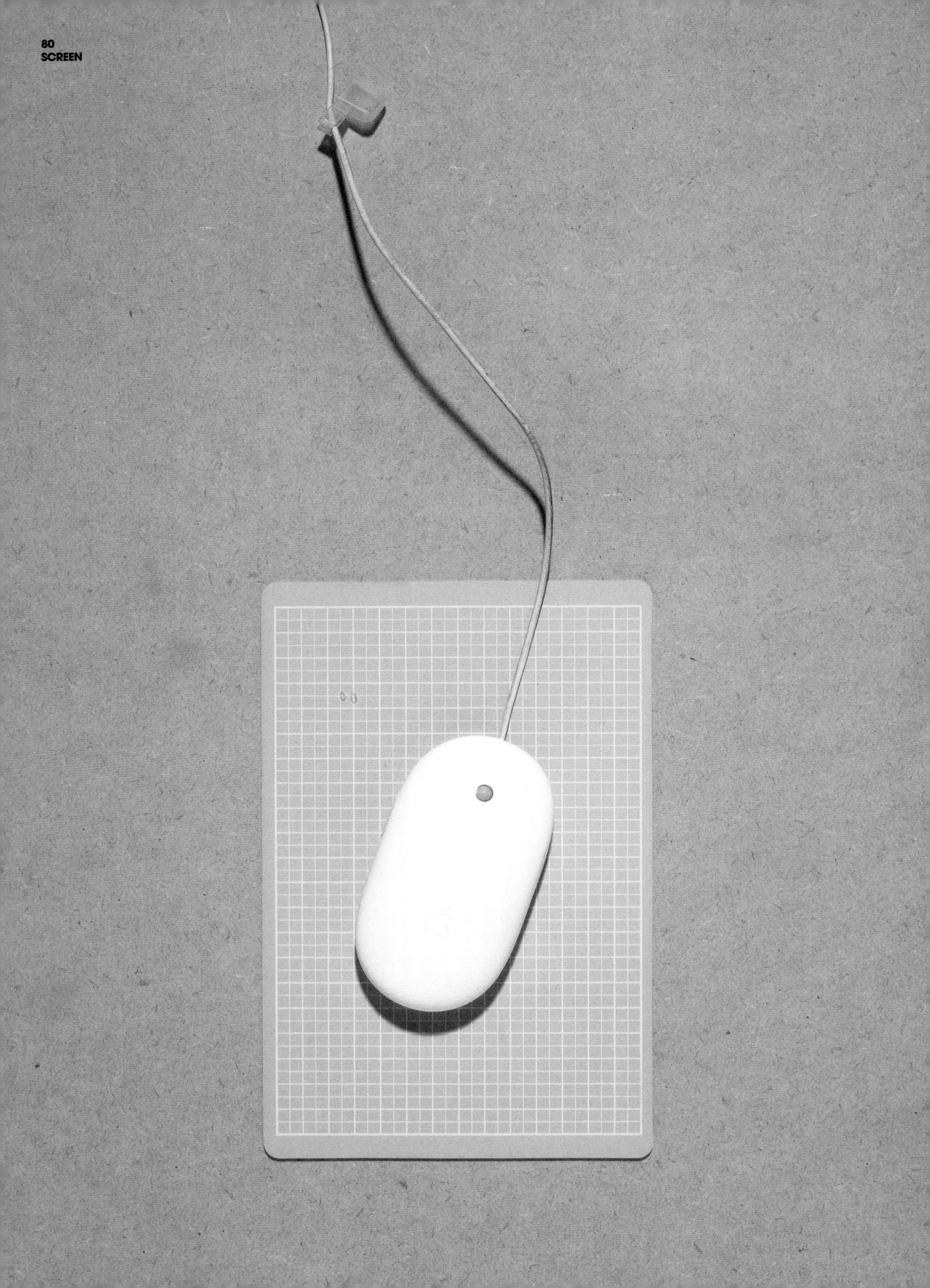

SCREEN

CRAIGLIST

I read somewhere that the design of craiglist.org will be changed in the UK because it doesn't look advanced enough to attract sufficient people to become as popular as it is in the USA. That would be an absolute shame. The html-based 'design' is a breath of fresh air and, in a way, shockingly simple (no ads) in a sea of animated and over-designed websites. *(Jop van Bennekom)*

www.craigslist.org

BATTLES PROMO

UVA music video for the new Battles single Tonto. The Power of LED. *(Joe Burrin)*

www.uva.co.uk

THE CADBURY'S GORILLA ADVERT

It still makes me smile. *(Kjell Ekhorn)*

www.aglassandahalffullproductions.com

FOREVER

Forever is a documentary by Heddy Honigmann about Père-Lachaise, the famous cemetery in Paris. We saw it on Dutch television, and it will be on our minds for years to come. In the documentary, the narrator interviews people visiting the graves of artists like Chopin, Proust and Apollinaire about the role of art in everyday life. By doing this, the documentary paints a beautiful image of the triangle that exists between art, life and death. Some of the characters are quite memorable (such as the embalmer who looks like he's about to burst into tears constantly, but reveals that he cannot physically cry, as he has defective tear glands—no greater metaphor for the human tragedy than that). One funny detail is that the most famous grave, that of Jim Morrison, is not featured in the documentary, but still quite present, in the form of hordes of lost Doors fans that you see wandering around in the background. *(Experimental Jetset)*

www.imdb.com/title/tt0906743

I-PHONE

Forget the Audi ad, or the MTV idents, I think the one piece of screen-based design that's had me giggling and jiggling about like a child has to be the Apple iPhone interface. Okay, maybe you need a five-year-old's finger grafted to the end of your own to use the keyboard function but, really, this is the only vision of the future I had in junior school finally made real. *(Jon Forss)*

www.apple.com/iphone

VVORK.

An endless and very addictive collection of nice projects. *(Martin Frostner)*

www.vvork.com

SHELLY BY JOHNNY KELLY

(Richard Hogg)

www.mickeyandjohnny.com

PLANET EARTH

Although it has been available elsewhere for a while, this was only released to the US audience this spring. The single most universally engaging documentary I've ever seen. *(Corey Holms)*

www.bbc.co.uk/nature/animals/planetearth/

IPHONE

I wasn't going to get one. Too expensive. Early versions always shit. Will get mugged. Etcetera. Etcetera. Then I went in the store, picked one up and did the zoomy-into-picture thing with finger and thumb. Yes please, Steve. The best bit is the calculator application. That is one sexy-looking $650 calculator. Sucker. *(Tom Phillips)*

www.apple.com/iphone

DE VOLKSKRANT.NL

Every week the De Volkskrant newspaper publishes on its website a comment by a designer or artist. This one by Lust charts the feeling in each state by the way it presents itself through its news. Move the cursor over country and a window opens to tell you more. It is brilliantly conceived. *(David Quay)*

http://extra.volkskrant.nl/oog/client/index.php?artworkId=127
http://www.lust.nl/oog/index.php?view=archive

OSMOTRONIC

Matthew Falla and his genius Interactive poster collaboration. *(Danny Sangra)*

www.osmotronic.com/interaphics

BAT FOR LASHES

Bat for Lashes video to their song What's a Girl to Do. *(Jens Schildt)*

www.colonelblimp.com/directors/dougalwilson

STYLE BUBBLE

I quite like this new blog:
http://stylebubble.typepad.com. *(Becky Smith)*

THIS IS ENGLAND.

Fantastic styling, soundtrack, script and acting in a film that's both funny and chilling.
(StudioThomson)

www.thisisenglandmovie.cc.uk

BAT FOR LASHES PROMO BY DOUGLAS WILSON

I think Douglas Wilson's been around a while and it shows because his work is so well put together and quietly very confident. This particular promo is beautifully simple, with a very subtle use of effects. I think it is one shot and the camera is static throughout, focusing on the singer, and then suddenly it moves away from her and standing in the road 'off camera' there is this odd little couple in fancy dress holding a balloon. They reminded me of a really sweet, sad Henri Rousseau painting of a Pierrot couple. I wonder if they were based on it? *(Rachel Thomas)*

www.colonelblimp.com/directors/dougalwilson/

FACEBOOK.

It's hard to not admit its greatness.
(Erik Torstensson)

www.facebook.com

DESIGNERS REPUBLIC'S QOOB WEBSITE.

(Robert Urquhart)

www.qoob.tv

THE LIVES OF OTHERS

A German-language film by director Florian Henckel von Donnersmarck about the Stasi secret police before the fall of the Berlin Wall. More engaging than anything Hollywood produced this year. *(YES Studio)*

www.sonyclassics.com/thelivesofothers

IT'S TIME FOR GRAFIK TO DON THE RED STRIDES AND FLUFFY BEARD AGAIN —HERE'S YOUR CHANCE TO GET YOUR HANDS ON SOME TOP-NOTCH GIVEAWAYS IN THIS MONTH'S EXTRA-SPECIAL OBJEKTS OF DESIRE…

CARHARTT

Two wheels good, four wheels bad, so the saying goes. But two wheels are even better when they're attached to this supercool BMX cruiser made by supercool streetwear providers Carhartt, and they're also a prize in this month's very special Objekts of Desire. All you have to do to get your hands on one is to tell us where Carhartt's fourth Kill the DJ event took place.
www.carhartt-streetwear.com

STEIDL BOOKS

Purveyors of some of the most covetable books around, which feature some of the most interesting content, Steidl's books are always exquisitely produced and immaculately designed. Here's your chance to get your hands on fifteen titles which have been handpicked for one fortunate Grafik reader by the lovely folks at SteidlMack in London. To win, just tell us which major photography book will be reissued by Steidl in May 2008.
www.steidlville.com

PRODUCT OF GOD

Walls looking a bit bare? Fret no more—here's your chance to win three gorgeous signed, limited-edition prints courtesy of the very generous people at Product of God, vendors of some of the finest prints from Big Photographic's very talented roster of artists and illustrators. To win all three (Geisha by Jasper Goodall, Kiss Me You Twat by Parra and Peacocks by Klaus Haapanemi), just tell us the print run of Jasper Goodall's Geisha.
www.productofgod.net

IITTALA

You don't need Grafik to tell you that Iittala produces some of the most mouth-watering homewares around. This year it showed us that Scandinavian design isn't just about cool minimalism with a magical collection of ceramics for the Taika series decorated by Finnish illustrator Klaus Haapanemi. Keep your eyes peeled for two brand-new colourways in 2008. To win the set shown here, just tell us who was responsible for designing the form of the Taika range.
www.iittala.com

COLETTE

If design-conscious visitors only have time to visit one shop in Paris, Colette usually wins hands-down for its jaw-dropping collections of must-have fashion, design, books and all-round gorgeous things. The very nice people at Colette HQ have given us three very covetable limited-edition scented candles created especially for the store by art director extraordinaire Fabien Baron for Mizensir. To get your hands on all three (go on—you know you want to), just tell us who was responsible for developing the scent for Monsieur Baron.
www.colette.fr

SEND YOUR ANSWERS TO GIVEAWAY@GRAFIKMAGAZINE.CO.UK BY 31 JANUARY 2008, AND DON'T FORGET TO INCLUDE FULL ADDRESS DETAILS.

Design Tshirts Store graniph

www.graniph.com

Another year, another crop of inspirational young things destined to ride the road to success thanks to boundless talent, originality and, Grafik hopes, a little editorial leg-up. We're keen to catch up with Talent's class of 07 and, not least, to have a gander at what they've been up to since we last met.

TALENT GALLERY

We'd like to reintroduce the photographers, illustrators, designers and rule-breakers who got us excited this year, and ask the question, "2007—How was it for you?" Watch this space for the next generation of creative upstarts in 2008. Enjoy.

CLAIRE SCULLY

This year saw the first Sanctuary of Wilderness exhibition with Susie Wright at the Illustration Gallery in Stroud. In preparation for this event, there was a lot of drawing and more cups of tea than could be imagined. While spending time freelancing, I have also spent a massive amount of time this year developing new pieces and pushing further ideas for my personal work. So, as 2008 approaches there will be new drawings to be hung in more exhibitions, also hopes of getting a studio/print workshop together, and inevitably more tea-drinking.

www.thequietrevolution.co.uk

```
Have's and Have Not's

197 AOC material
201 wemadethat KX
202 Ruby Quince
203 grafik images
204 Helena Blackman logo/site
205 boy cried wolf
206 Uniguild card / Webupdate
207 APFEL february 07
208 storms T&H
209 day four
210 Gort Scott
211 AOC business card
212 APFEL march 07
213 Bastion Host
214 CR supplement
215 APFEL april 07
216 Tom Brown Website
217 APFEL may 07
218 DD films
219 smutlane jewellery
220 APFEL
```

STEPHEN OSMAN

Have's and Have Not's

I have started at A Practice for Everyday Life
I have given a talk at Camberwell College of Art
I have been shortlisted for an RIBA competition with We
Made That and Nick Wood

I have not bought that new bike
I have not had enough sleep
I have not been to Moscow

www.eyeohhewe.co.uk

INGE SCHOUTSEN

The year 2007 started with an audio project in the
Dominican Republic, interviewing Dutch prisoners
sentenced for years because of drug trafficking. I then
explored the world of online dating by portraying the
members of the Positive Connection, a dating site for
people living with HIV/AIDS. The year will end with
documenting Orania, a white South African enclave
solely for Boers/Afrikaners. In between I made a series
about foundlings, abandoned at birth but since
grown-up. 2007 was the year of deepening my
documentary approach and discovering new media
through experiments with film.

www.ingeschoutsen.nl

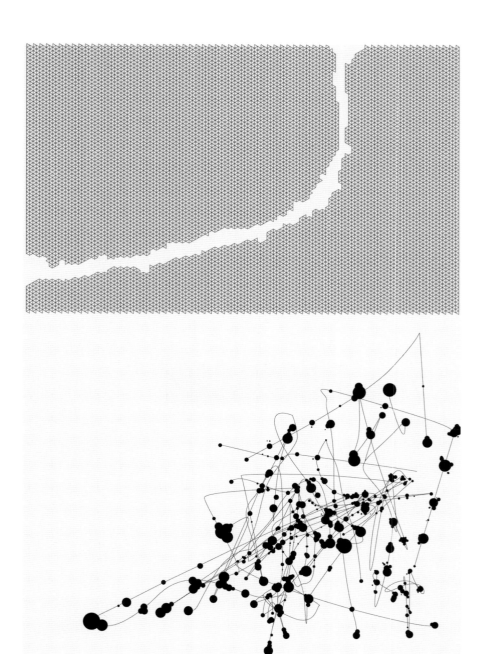

NIC HUGHES

My 2007 has been defined almost entirely by two research projects for Nokia ComLab. Unfortunately, I'm NDA'd to the hilt and can't say any more than that. These images are contributions for a book coming out next year. I'm trying to explore system-based methods of production. Presently, I'm excited by the possibility that the mobile phone could be more significant than the Gutenberg press—increasingly mobile devices are 'authoring' and editing reality. Equally, I'm fascinated by virtual environments and their ability to act as 'hyperstitional' locations: that is, fictional spaces that feed back and disturb 'the real'.

nic@vaux.net

EVA KELLENBERGER

At the beginning of the year I locked myself in a room and made my portfolio to apply for a Masters at the RCA; it was worth it, I just started there. Apart from applications, I worked for four months on a cookbook, 1080 Recipes, for Phaidon Press, and made a catalogue with two architects who have been appointed by the RIBA to collaborate with school kids. After that I drove down to Italy, Croatia, Montenegro and Slovenia and all the way back to Switzerland. It was nice.

www.evakellenberger.com

DANIEL SANNWALD

2007 was cool like ice cream and the plan for 2008 is to be out to lunch forever.

www.danielsannwald.com

BRYONY BIRKBECK

2007 slapped me round the face. But in a good way.

www.bryonybirkbeck.com

RICHARD SARSON

Words 0–13 I am given no more than 100 words by Grafik to describe 2007. 14–30 are filled with possibilities, potential and hard work in my first year as an RCA graduate. 31–45 used recounting the group show I was involved with at Nettie Horn gallery (thanks, Ellen). 46–78 on client-driven projects including wall graphics based on global office locations for infrastructure consultancy Faber Maunsell whilst working at OPX (www.opx.co.uk) and freelance work for Exhibit Gallery. 79–100 used looking forward to 2008, the unknown adventures it will bring and finally wishing a happy New Year to everyone graphically challenged.

www.richardsarson.com

MARCUS GAAB

This year was: Many air miles. A baby. NY NY. Lovely assistants. Berlin. New agents. JOBS! Almost bankrupt. No sleep. No phone ringing for weeks. Her name is Zarah. A long car repair. A big house indoors. An apartment getting too small. A studio almost too big. Art. Royalty. Few boat rides. Hot weekends. Freezing on set in summer. FOOD! White nights. A dark daylight studio. No air miles spent. Finally making it into fancy hotels. No sports car again. A new haircut. A new body. Old clients. No new clients. Too much gear. No tuxedo. Hopefully making it to go skiing. BIG budgets. No fees. A very usual year.

www.marcusgaab.com

BEN FREEMAN

2007 has been a voyage of self-discovery. I went looking for myself in Morocco, Spain, Switzerland and Slovenia. I think I found myself but I'm going back to Slovenia to double-check. My conclusion? I might explore the role of the designer as publisher, editor or journalist. It also slowly started to dawn on me that no one outside of the cliquey world of graphic design gives a shit about us anymore (this is true, ask them) so I'm looking for a sexier job title—maybe property magnate or tycoon.

www.ben-freeman.com

ELIN SVENSSON

729 cups of tea consumed over twelve projects. One hard-drive failure and a lot less hair. The end of my second year on my BA and the beginning of my third and last. The sunny spring, the rainy summer, thin and thick sweaters worn under grey skies, blue skies, pink skies, scribbling, cutting, pasting, all day long, all night long, all week and year. Built paper chairs, folded dog ears and printed viruses. Thought about getting a tattoo, but didn't. Maybe next year.

www.elinsvensson.com

JETHRO HAYNES

My 2007 was a year of… confusion, conundrums, harebrained schemes, potentially hazardous practices, concussion, acupuncture, new horizons, unlikely job offers, self-indulgence, fortune, frustration, musical friends, too much TV, hoping for change, relaxing in style, working for free, paying the price, battling wills, hobby trade-offs, taking charge, learning daily, friendly strangers, old ghosts, broken backs, borrowed DVDs, constant care, lack of respect, terrible guilt, homelessness, too many painkillers, physiotherapy, MRIs, borrowed time, crime-scene investigation, hot and cold showers, old futures, new pasts.

www.jethrohaynes.com

VANIA ZOURAVLIOV

2007 was a good year for me. I worked on commercial projects for National Geographic, Sky TV and Omega watches as well as producing more personal drawings for Die Gestalten Verlag and Japanese magazine Yaso.

www.bigactive.com

AHONEN & LAMBERG

For us the year 2007 is the beginning; it is our first year as
Ahonen & Lamberg. Well, what can we say but true
clichés: it has been extraordinary, like falling in love.

www.ahonenandlamberg.com

NACHO ALEGRE

2007 has been a brilliant year, but never as good as 2008.

www.nachoalegre.com

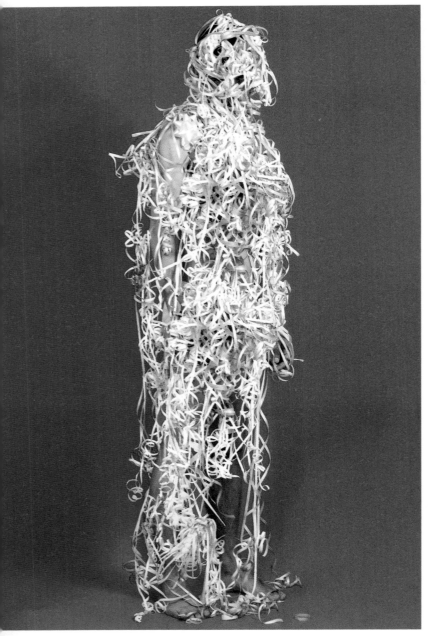

OLIVIA FRÉMINEAU

2007 was rock'n'roll, with ups and downs, but a great year and very challenging. I worked with beautiful, fascinating and talented people. Also 2007 was the first year I made a living by myself as a photographer. I survived the rabbit—he did not kill me—and I look forward to 2008 with curiosity, enthusiasm and lots of hope.

www.oliviafremineau.com

CHRISTOPHER THOMPSON

It's been an insane year full of many ends and new beginnings. Still finding my feet after graduating this year from Glasgow and relocating to London to start work with the fantastic team at MadeThought. Hopefully 2008 will bring the confidence to ride the unforgiving streets of the London rush hour on a fixed gear.

www.withalltenfingers.com

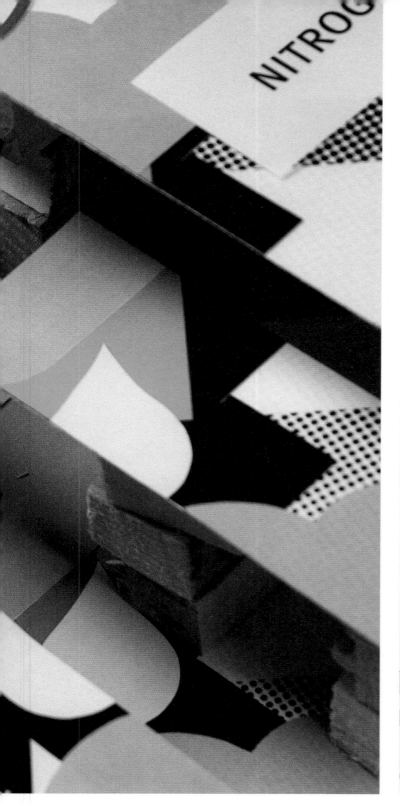

KATE MOROSS

2007 allowed me to officially call this my career. I have realised a handful of my life goals in these last twelve months alone. I have had to travel light years to keep up with the pace that my work requires. We all know how quickly the need for graphic design is changing. It seems everyone wants to be branded or rebranded—which has meant non-stop work and a constantly evolving aesthetic. Each person wants 'new', and it's a rat race to keep up, but so far I have managed it.

www.katemoross.com

CATHERINE GUIRAL

2007 was a good year. Quentin Walesch and I
collaborated and interacted. So did new people with
us. And we moved. To Berlin. The future will be happy.

Très Belle Année. Frohes Neues Jahr.

www.3n17.de

HANNAH WALDRON

I have spent the last few months since graduating creating the world of Hidden Places, a name under which future creations will live. I have been endeavouring to get the many ideas out of my head and laying the foundations of future projects including a forthcoming exhibition with fellow Brighton graduate Charlie Duck and a new book which I will be self-publishing in the New Year. I am enjoying meeting strangers wearing my owl and polar bear badges. I am excited about future possibilities.

www.hannahwaldron.co.uk

BEN RAYNER

2007 has treated me well. Been away, been at home,
and never too far from my cameras. Roll on 2008.

www.benrayner.com

Above: Fehler + Fairchild Semiconductor | 100 Days [Iraq Conflict 20.05.06 - 27.08.06] (Detail)

fallt

Various Artists | Format
MP3 + Offset Lithography
As music moves from LP to CD to MP3, what next for packaging, so long central to the music industry? 'Format', a new series delivered via Grafik, explores alternative audio/visual distribution models: printed inserts (free), downloadable audio (free), silkscreened CDRs (purchased).

Challenging the music industry not to abandon packaging, audio will be available for free download in MP3 format from January 2008.

www.fallt.com/format

Various Artists | Offset
Giclée Prints
Repurposing advertising space within a variety of publications, 'Offset' continues Fallt Publishing's long-standing investigation of different distribution media for various works. Free works inserted in advertising spaces are coupled with archival quality giclée prints in limited editions.

Recent works include: 'Crash', a drawing dictated by market forces; and '100 Days', a stark graphic depicting daily civilian death tolls in Iraq.

www.fallt.com/offset/100

INSIGHT
PAPER

IN THIS ISSUE'S INSIGHT, WE LOOK AT FOUR VERY DIFFERENT PROJECTS, ALL OF WHICH ALL USE PAPER TO BEAUTIFUL EFFECT.

ZOE BRADLEY/ARJOWIGGINS

Artist Zoe Bradley used paper to dramatic effect at an installation in New York's Girbaud SoHo store earlier this year. Entitled The Hanging Gardens of Pulp, the exhibition celebrated the decade-long tradition of fashion and textile innovation of designers Marithe+François Girbaud. Renowned for her paper pieces which are used for installations for fashion shoots and window displays, Bradley employed origami techniques to create supersized flowers and foliage which cascaded across the boutique's angular ceiling. Various different papers from both the Arjowiggins Curious Collection and Pop'Set range were intricately folded and then sewn together. The Hanging Gardens of Pulp was launched at an exhibition curated by Sebastien Agneessens (Formavision) and produced by ReflexAdvertising NY. Bradley also created a limited-edition line of paper origami headpieces to mark the exhibition launch.

www.arjowiggins.com
www.areia.com

2

3

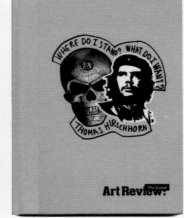

4

2 JOHN ROSS/GF SMITH

Photographer John Ross is not generally known for non-studio work, but some spare time on a trip to the Isle of Islay led to a beautiful series of shots of the bleak, prehistoric landscapes that demanded to be seen outside the confines of his workspace. Long-time collaborators SEA created an oversized book to show off the photographs, and paper for the project was supplied by GF Smith, with print from Team. The book uses Zen, a textured stock perfect for the tritones and dense black of the images. To contrast with the starkness of the images, the slipcase features double-hit fluoro yellow ink and pearlescent foil. An edition of 2,000 was printed, with 500 signed and numbered by the photographer.

www.gfsmith.com
www.seadesign.co.uk

3 AMANDA COUCH/DENMAUR PAPERS

Through the Looking Glass took place in Standard Life's Building 100 in London's Docklands in summer 2007. Curated by ARTed, the event featured twelve female artists who had been invited to make works in response to the still largely male-dominated surroundings. Performance artist and RCA graduate Amanda Couch has made items out of different substrates, but has recently used paper to make items such as baths, aprons,

dresses and curtains. For this event, Couch created a massive skirt made from over 200 metres of silk-coated paper (normally used for web offset printing). The paper was donated by Denmaur Papers, which also provided the substrate material for the thirty-two-page catalogue, with Amadeus Silk 170gsm and 250gsm being used for text and cover respectively.

www.denmaur.com

4 ART REVIEW ANNUAL/FENNER PAPER

Art Review has published its 2007/2008 annual showcasing the work of critically acclaimed Swiss artist Thomas Hirschhorn. The limited-edition publication examines his aspirations and motivations through collages of text and image, answering the questions "Where do I stand? What do I want?" The book uses a combination of different stocks. Ninety-six pages are devoted to Hirschhorn's collaged piece, and at the back of the annual is a calendar section for up-and-coming art shows—this is printed on Fenner's Omnia, an uncoated, tactile stock which gives bulk without adding weight. The annual was printed by St Ives Roche and is linenbound using a striking yellow cloth, with black foiled text on the back cover.

www.fennerpaper.co.uk
www.art-review.com

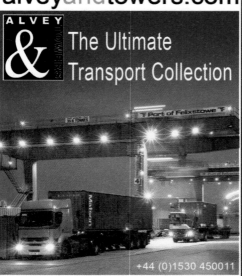

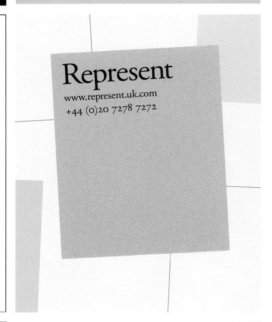

FUTURE OBJECT
FUTURE CONNECT
FUTURE SELECT
FUTURE DIALECT
FUTURE PROSPECT
FUTURE ELECT
FUTURE DIRECT
FUTURE SUSPECT
FUTURE EFFECT
FUTURE INFECT
FUTURE REJECT
FUTURE PERFECT

RESULTS FROM OUR COMPETITION:
"Letters form words that convey
meanings that can make pictures,"
the late great Alan Fletcher once
remarked. He was talking
specifically about his
found-letter compositions but also
making a broader observation about
that power words have to inflame
the imagination and create mental
pictures. Good graphic design,
after all, is as much about words
as it is about pictures, so during
2007 we teamed up with the
dedicated souls at Designers Are
Wankers to seek out new design
writing talent.

When the entries to our Future
Perfect competition began
pouring in we were hugely satisfied
to discover that there are a lot of
designers out there with something
to get off their chest. Our five
writing briefs inspired some
passionate invective as well as
some very thoughtful writing. Power
to the word.

Our panel of judges (Jonathan Bell,
Richard Bucht, Susanna Edwards,
John Jervis, Angharad Lewis, Lee
McCormack, Mark Owens, Mark Porter,
Caroline Roberts and Robert
Urquhart) have carefully studied
the entries and we're very happy to
announce our winner and three
runners-up:

WINNER: Anthony Noel
RUNNER-UP 1: Holly Wales
RUNNER-UP 2: David Garavin
RUNNER-UP 3: Adam Cohen

Congratulations to Anthony, who
bags himself a writing
assignment in Grafik, an Apple
MacBook, a regular column on
Designersarewankers.com, dinner
with a Designersarewankers.com guru
of his choice, a library of
essential design books and a
subscription to Grafik. Phew,
that's quite a prize and a very
deserving winner.

Well done also to our runners-up,
whose winning entries will all be
published on designersarewankers.
com and who also get a subscription
to Grafik and a selection of design
books, including Lee McCormack's
cult title Designers Are Wankers.

And now over to Anthony and his
winning article...

Designers
are
wankers.com

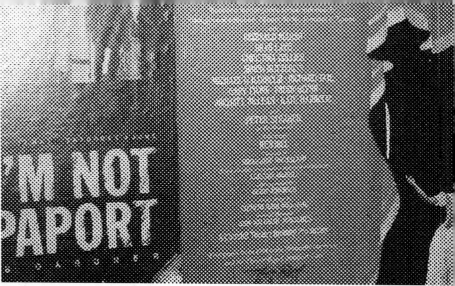

GRAPHIC DESIGN'S BEST KEPT SECRET (ISN'T SO SECRET ANYMORE)

BY ANTHONY NOEL

Nestling stage left of Bristol's Old Vic Theatre it's easy to miss the inconspicuous green door to La Taverna dell Artista. Behind it, a warren of hallways leads through to the small independent restaurant that's been run by the Renato family for nearly thirty years.

Renato's, as all the locals know it, is an unexpected place to find a shrine to design—but maybe that was not the intention. Growing up in the shadow of the Old Vic, Renato's is a theatrical establishment through and through. Siblings George and Angela took over running the restaurant a couple of years ago from their parents, who founded the business in the early Eighties. It was they who transformed Renato's from a grimy, low nighttime dive called The Stage Door.

The Renato family moved in when it had reached its nadir, and it was while contemplating the lowest and darkest of the medieval rooms that they had their Changing Rooms moment. Their collection of theatre posters, gathered initially on noticeboards and then kept through a combination of archival urges and a growing love of the medium, might be better appreciated brightening the walls of their new restaurant.

Almost three decades later not a whole lot has changed. Stuff has been ripped off (literally, not by idea-starved desperadoes), drawn on, defaced and generally left unloved. Occasionally something is replaced. Certain areas are now into their third layer. (How refreshing it is to talk of layers in a context far away from Photoshop.) Nonetheless, Renato's owner George talks fluently

and passionately about the collection. He even considers some of the graffiti pretty inspired, like the extra facial details on the Harvey poster. Angela, meanwhile, mourns the lack of respect their clientele pay to these historical artefacts. Given that Bristol is home to the infamous Banksy, they might regard themselves as having got off lightly. The fact is, whatever Angela might think, these aren't museum pieces.

The design world should be grateful, and not a little chastened, that they felt compelled to share their enjoyment and appreciation of the poster. We're too quick to sneer when non-designers encroach on our turf, wincing at Word Art and dreading our clients' comments when it comes to presentation time. We know what skills have gone into producing our work, to what level of detail we have applied ourselves, how insightfully we have interpreted the brief. We are, quite rightly, proud, and this is a good thing. But we can forget that our work has a life beyond our creative effort, and that others have an interest, and usually an investment, in what we do.

The collection at Renato's has been compiled by design consumers, not connoisseurs. The restaurant's other proudly displayed collection is of framed, signed actors' portraits. (Oh, and one of Graham Gooch. But as cricket won't be shoehorned neatly into my tale, we'll not mention it again.) What makes Renato's an enlightening experience for graphic designers is that the editing process goes through a different set of filters to the one we would use ourselves. The criteria for a place

on Renato's walls can have as much to do with sentiment or humour or a desire to record a historical event as it might aesthetic reasons. It feels like consumer power in action. Any other curator, especially a design professional, would have grouped the work according to a system that designers would understand. There would be stylistic themes and artificially imposed relationships. The opportunity to match posters for The Tempest and Return to the Forbidden Planet (essentially Shakespeare in space) would be too much for me to pass up, but here the need to cover a damaged patch probably took priority.

To sit in this room, in the presence of nearly forty years (in one case over seventy years) of design, is to be reminded that people other than designers can appreciate graphic design for more than the technique and craft involved. This isn't the place to start nodding knowingly about kerning, or looking closely at the bezier curves. So, while it has plenty to offer designers, from a wonderful poster for a wildlife film festival to some great hand-rendered type and lots of great ideas, the best thing about Renato's, from a designer's point of view, is the sense that you are entering a world of design, but through a door you wouldn't normally use. It's appropriate, then, that Renato's used to be called The Stage Door. These posters have been collected not because of their design, but because of their function in the business of putting on a show. It's a useful reminder that graphic design is not an outcome, but merely another cog in a machine that, to most of the paying public, works behind the scenes.

Viewpoint
2007—How was it for you?

John Warwicker, Tomato
www.tomato.co.uk

Busy. And then even more so. My second year of living in Australia and at last being able to use my painting studio here to make work (at least for the Underworld album project). One of the highlights of the year was helping organise and curate an exhibition of the Tokyo Type Directors Club here in Melbourne (at Monash University) and in Sydney (UTS). The other highlight has been my involvement in Underworld's new album and its surrounding projects.

David Bailey, Kiosk
www.letskiosk.com

David is… pleased he saw Mastodon, Brakes, Lamb of God, Black Keys, Julian Cope, Carl Craig, Foo Fighters, Goldie, Andy C, Black Devil Disco Club, KTL; … glad to have met Julian Cope, Goldie, Stephen O'Malley, Wolfgang Flur, Enter Shikari, Barry Miles; … remembering Lisbon, San Sebastian, Bilbao, Antigua; … proud to have contributed to Helvetica50, Grafik, Bend in the River, Sheffield City Centre, Stolen Music Collective, Sheffield Uni design students' minds; … unsettled by amount of time spent on Facebook. David Bailey and 2008 are now friends.

Daniel Eatock
www.eatock.com

The deadline for writing this short text about how it was for me in 2007 was Friday 26 October: this is two months and five days before the end of 2007. If you asked Kimi Raikkonen how it was for him in 2007, with 18 per cent of the F1 Grand Prix season remaining, he would have had a very different answer than he would at the end of his season. I have sixty-six out of 365 days left and, like Kimi, am looking forward to an extraordinarily happy ending to the year in Brazil.

Michael Pybus
www.michaelpybus.co.uk

I've got no complaints. Well, actually, I've got loads but that's just because I like to moan. Life really ain't that bad. So I'm gonna try and be a good person and bookend the year with something almost optimistic. It was OK.

Emmi
www.emmi.co.uk

In twelve:
Industrious
Academic
Open
Awarding
Inspirational
Fun
Significant
Confused
Focused
Collective
Decisive
Encouraging

Damien Poulain
www.damienpoulain.com

It started like any other year, with a grey January, quiet for the whole winter, then came spring with its light clothes and new projects. I have met really nice people through work and collaborated with amazing ones who made me rethink my practice. It was also my fifth year in London, the year of my sister's first baby, and there were a few nice trips to various destinations in Europe. It was pink, red and white, blue and yellow, quite a colourful year and a successful one in terms of colour palette.

Mat Fowler, Playarea
www.play-area.co.uk

Mat Fowler

First I went to my friends till the New
Year started, and then I went to Butlins
to see lots of bands and a funfair,
and then I picked vegetables in
the garden and then, we made big
wooden letters spelling Pointer, and
then I drew some logos for a shop, and
then I saw a mouse, in the studio and
then I played guitar with some friends,
and we had drinks, and then I went to
bed, and then I woke up not
feeling well.

Alex Bec
www.alexbec.com

ALEX BEC

Jaded
Frivolous
Magic
Arduous
Meaningful
Jovial
Jubilant
Appetising
Sleepless
Occupational
Necessary
Domestic
Happy 2008. x

Anthony Burrill
www.friendchip.com

At the start of 2007 I was hoping for
a massive musical revolution, along
the lines of punk rock or acid house.
Years ending in a seven have got a
good track record for this kind of thing.
Unfortunately all we got were Klaxons
and the Spice Girls reunion. Perhaps
the revolution will start in 2008 instead.

Anna Rhodes
www.eatcake.co.uk

Anna

I acquired a degree, my first pot
plant and a yellow pencil. I built a
giant coin-operated giraffe ride and
showed it in four exhibitions. Hoodwink
is now my favourite word. I discovered
Dostoevsky (on audio tape) and
watched Patti Smith do Horses at the
Roundhouse. I couldn't live without
Akkurat, Akzidenz or Baskerville. I
dined at Maxims in Paris and Testes in
Stoke Newington. I fell in love. I'd like to
thank Robin, Aoife, Laura, GTS, Frank
Cartledge, Mum and Gwyneth Paltrow
for being a constant inspiration. 9/10.

Matt Willey, Studio 8
www.studio8design.co.uk

Matthew Willey

Most things that I thought happened
this year actually happened in 2006.
My memory doesn't seem to hold
on to the dates as well as it used to.
The things that I know happened this
year include: my son turning one, my
daughter starting school, jumping off
some rocks into the sea somewhere
near Stockholm, seeing our friends
in San Francisco and The Sopranos
ending.

Maxlot
www.maxalot.com

If you like being a wandering nomad
(which we do), then 2007 was a
hoot! After wintering in New York, we
returned to Maxalot Barcelona, our
big bang exhibition with the Parisian
über-charmer WK Interact himself.
From bustling Barcelona to the Dutch
seaside town of Scheveningen
(don't try and pronounce that
without Strepsils to hand) whence we
controlled our empire for the summer.
And as the leaves turn to brown there's
only one place left to go: hasta Miami
piquante art action.

Viewpoint
2007—How was it for you?

Matt Pyke, Universal Everything
www.universaleverything.com

How was it for me?
(Religious) Row 14 of the iPhone
Launch, San Francisco
(Proud) Speaking to audiences about
AdvancedBeauty.org
(Foolish) Eating carrot foam at Green
Zebra, Chicago
(Gosh) Seeing Britney, 50 Cent and
Kanye hanging with our MTV Award
Show graphics
(Colossal) Standing on top of Win Hill,
Ladybower Reservoir, Peak District
(Sharp) Seven days working with only
a pencil
(Defiant) Loving the London 2012 logo
before its launch

Hector Pottie, Third Eye
www.thirdeyedesign.co.uk

2007 for me has been about
broadening my horizons and stepping
out of my comfort zone.
New city
New home
New studio
New team
New clients
New destinations
New experiences
New influences
New friends
New family
Jam-packed and non-stop.
A little bit scary at times, continually
surprising, totally rewarding.
Forward ever, backward never.
Explore explore explore.

Will Hudson
www.willhudson.co.uk

For me, 2007 has been the year
everything has finally come together.
Graduating from Brighton in June
kickstarted a busy second half of the
year. Third Eye Design is proving to be
an exciting place to develop as a
designer and If You Could and It's Nice
That are both gathering momentum
to take into next year. Roll on 2008.

Jon Sueda & Gail Swanlund, Stripe
www.stripela.com

2007 was a year of lots of shifts, big and
small. It was a year of working on a lot
of books… I'm not sure why people ask
us to do so many books.
It was a year of working with smart,
interesting clients like Michael Ned
Holte, a year of collaborative work, a
year of making tiny sweet objects and
huge whipped-up happenings.
From our treehouse studio we could
watch storms rolling in or the sky
turning gold over the mountains. Or we
spied on the friendly local fauna doing
what critters do best.
And it was also a year of good
'regulars'—we took daily hikes to
procure a cup of coffee or to Armon's
Café to chat with Lin and dine on 'the
usual', then headed back to make
things by lantern-light.
Seems like we never had a chance to
take it easy.

Gerard Saint, Big Active
www.bigactive.com

"How was it for you?" Just like the
awkward silence the morning after
a night's indiscretion, looking back
on the year that was is a little bit like
avoiding eye contact with a one-night
stand while combing a hangover out
of your hair—you know everything will
be much clearer one way or the other,
but not for a good few hours. This year
along the way we picked up a few
D&AD pencils, worked with The Enemy,
competed with Athlete, explored
Architecture in Helsinki, shot Alison
Goldfrapp, and scored some Ibiza
Rocks. We worked hard, and partied
hard, and helped keep the bar staff in
wages at the Griffin Pub in Shoreditch.
So pretty much business as usual, I think.
It's hard to be objective when it's all still
so close—ask me about it again next
year once the Nurofen's kicked in.

Sanderson Bob
www.sandersonbob.com

More so this year I have noticed the
capabilities we all possess. We have
the power to inspire, motivate, dream.
I would like to take this opportunity
to thank everyone that I have been
involved with throughout 2007 who has
the genuine milk of human kindness
running through their veins. You have
given me extra motivation. Inspired me
without knowing. Given my dreams
legs.